the
woodworker's
solution book

the woodworker's *solution* book

Over 200 answers to your top woodworking problems

ALAN AND GILL BRIDGEWATER

POPULAR WOOD WORKING BOOKS

Cincinnati, Ohio

A QUARTO BOOK

First published in North America in 1998 by
Popular Woodworking Books
an imprint of F&W Publications, Inc.,
1507 Dana Avenue
Cincinnati, OH 45207
1-800/289-0963

ISBN 1-55870-496-5

This book was published by
Quarto Publishing plc
6 Blundell Street
London N7 9BH

Senior art editor: Penny Cobb
Designer: Glyn Bridgewater
Woodwork demonstrations: Charles Camp,
Ace Restoration
Illustrators: Gill Bridgewater,
Glyn Bridgewater
Photographer: Paul Forrester
Picture researcher: Miriam Hyman
Senior editor: Sally MacEachern
Text editor: Robert Runck
Editorial director: Pippa Rubinstein
Art director: Moira Clinch

Typeset by Central Southern
Typesetters, Eastbourne
Manufactured by
Eray Scan Pte Ltd, Singapore
Printed by Star Standard Industries (Pte)
Ltd, Singapore

Contents

9 I have managed to get some good wood at a good price, but it is too thin. I have a project that requires thicker stock. Can you come up with a good laminating design to make wood thicker?

sol.1 Interlocking joint
sol.2 Veneer strip laminating

10 I have built a small chest. I don't think brass hinges look right on it. I would like to use wooden hinges. Is it too late at this stage? Can you come up with a couple of designs?

sol.1 Integral dovetail hinge
sol.2 Laminated surface hinge

Sawing 30

11 I am cutting four tenons. I have cut two already, and they are loose and sloppy. How can I make them tight and good-looking? And how can I cut good tenons the next time?

sol.1 Gluing shims
sol.2 Correct use of the mortise gauge
sol.3 Correct way to mark the shoulder line
sol.4 Ways to achieve good joints

12 I am trying to cut out identical pieces with a scroll saw. The saw vibrates a great deal, so every piece I cut out is slightly different. How can I adjust the saw? How can I make sure all the pieces are identical?

sol.1 Installing and adjusting the saw
sol.2 Sandwich cutting
sol.3 Cutting tight angles
sol.4 Cutting thicker stock

13 I have just cut some wood to make a box. The ends of the pieces are rough and ragged. How can I fix them? How can I avoid doing this the next time?

sol.1 Removing the sharp edge
sol.2 Ways of making a better cut

Planing 36

14 My planer is cutting a rough surface. What is the best method of planing a piece of wood to avoid a rough-looking finish?

sol.1 Check out the wood
sol.2 Gauging moisture content
sol.3 Servicing planer knives and tables
sol.4 Overall adjustments

15 I have just finished hand-planing a piece of end grain, and the grain split off! How do I fix it? And how do I avoid splitting end grain when planing?

sol.1 Glue repair
sol.2 Using a supporting block
sol.3 Adjusting a block plane
sol.4 Cutting a miter
sol.5 Planing at a skewed angle

16 I put several boards through the planer, and they are all slightly rippled. How can I redo them?

sol.1 Adjusting the cutterhead
sol.2 Safely feeding the workpiece
sol.3 Checking the belts
sol.4 Using a smoothing plane
sol.5 Using a cabinet scraper

17 I want to build a table from quarter-sawn white oak, but it is very expensive! Also, I am worried that the 4 x 4 in. solid legs might split and/or warp. How can I do the project less expensively? And how can I ensure that the legs stay true?

sol.1 Hollow quarter-sawn mitered legs
sol.2 Laminated legs
sol.3 Hollow legs covered with hand-sawn veneers

Chisels 46

18 My chisels are digging in and going off-line—to the extent that I have made a very bad, loose through tenon. How can I repair the tenon? What am I doing wrong?

sol.1 Avoid making large cuts
sol.2 Packing a tenon
sol.3 Anatomy of a chisel
sol.4 Common chisel types
sol.5 Using a chisel

19 I have botched one half of a half-lap—it is too deep. How can I cut the other half to fit?

sol.1 Cutting the other half to compensate
sol.2 Controlled paring
sol.3 Cutting in from the sides
sol.4 Skimming

20 I have just cut a bad dovetail—it is too loose. How can I compensate to make it fit? How can I avoid the problem the next time?

sol.1 Veneering a loose dovetail
sol.2 Basic open dovetails
sol.3 Sliding dovetails
sol.4 Blind miter dovetail

21 I am making a frame, and have broken the tenon off in the mortise. How can I remove the broken stub? How can I repair the joint?

sol.1 Fitting a stub tenon
sol.2 Convert to a bolt and toggle fitting

Routers 54

22 I am having a hard time with my router doing decorative edge cuts freehand. Is there a better way?

sol.1 Use templates and template guides
sol.2 Build your own subbase

23 In cutting with my router, I find myself burning the edges. How can I remove the burn marks? What went wrong?

sol.1 Overcutting
sol.2 Sharpening
sol.3 Checking for a buildup of resin and debris
sol.4 Checking the direction and rate of feed
sol.5 Turret stops

24 I have butt-jointed two boards. The seam does not look good. What can I do to improve it?

sol.1 Routing a cover-up groove
sol.2 Routing a channel for a decorative inlay
sol.3 Routing a dovetail groove

Joints 60

25 I have just made a drawer using dowel joints. It and I are coming apart at the seams! Where am I going wrong? How can I repair the damage?

sol.1 Designing dowel joints correctly
sol.2 Use of dovetails
sol.3 Redesign
sol.4 Using reinforcements

26 I am making a large number of dowel joints. I have drilled the holes too deep—and some deeper than others! I need to ensure accuracy and consistency of dowel depth. And I need to make sure it doesn't happen again. How?

sol.1 Using a drill press depth stop
sol.2 Using a tape mark or a stop collar
sol.3 Making a stop block
sol.4 Making a depth jig

27 I have installed a doorframe casing with mitered joints. The only problem is that the joints keep opening and closing with changing humidity. How can I stop this?

sol.1 Paint or varnish to stop shrinkage
sol.2 Cutting through the joint
sol.3 Installing a decorative trim

28 **sol.4** Adding corner blocks
I made a plank tabletop and it has warped. How can I correct the warping? Is it possible to avoid warping in future projects?

sol.1 Seasoning of wood
sol.2 Selecting the right cut and alternating the grain
sol.3 Sliding screw battens
sol.4 Sliding dovetail dado

Sanding and Scraping 70

29 I have just sanded an edge profile and it does not look very good. How can I fix it up? What is the best way of sanding such a profile?

sol.1 Making a backing block
sol.2 Making a mini drum sander for the drill press
sol.3 Making a disk pivot jig

30 I just finished making a table. Unfortunately I dropped my hand plane on it, and now there is a sizable dent in the surface. How can I repair it?

sol.1 Steaming
sol.2 Clear filler
sol.3 Wax filler
sol.4 Veneer patch

Glues and Clamps 74

31 I have a beautiful chair—all glued together. But now that the glue has set, I find that the frame is misaligned! How can I correct the problem?

sol.1 Using bar clamps
sol.2 Steaming and disassembling
sol.3 Using a rope
sol.4 Making corner clamps
sol.5 Checking for square
sol.6 Leveling chair legs

32 I am ready to start making slab seats for Windsor chairs—and all but one of my clamps are being used on another job. What can I do?

sol.1 Rubbed joints
sol.2 Cross-screw clamps
sol.3 Using dogs

33 I glued up a bed end, and it is out of square. Why did this happen? How can I disassemble it and make sure this doesn't happen again?

sol.1 Checking joints and regluing the frame
sol.2 Drilling out the dowels and steaming
sol.3 Reverse clamping
sol.4 Squaring up the frame

34 I have assembled a small box. Glue dribbles have ruined the surface. Can I repair the damage? How can I avoid the problem in the future?

sol.1 Disassemble and scrape
sol.2 Surface preparation
sol.3 How to minimize gluing problems

Construction 84

35 I am making a chair that has round, tapered spindles. My lathe is out of action —how can I make the spindles without using a lathe?

sol.1 Using a drawknife
sol.2 Working with a knife and spokeshave

36 My workshop is short of space. I need an easily made fold-up table for gluing. Have you any ideas?

sol.1 Folding wall table
sol.2 Norwegian klapboard
sol.3 Sawhorse table
sol.4 Gateleg table

Wood Finishing 94

Handtool Care 104

Keeping up Power Tools 112

Glossary, Index and Credits 126

Introduction

Sometimes when I'm alone in my garden-shed workshop—at the end of a long day when a project has gone particularly well—I sit down in my old armchair, and have a good, long and hard look at whatever project is in the making. I let my mind drift over the various pleasures and problems that have taken up the day. It's a wonderfully uplifting feeling, as my tired body unwinds and my mind relives the various challenges and successes.

But of course it's not all joy. There are times when the day seems to have been one long, uphill slog. I'm sure you know what I mean—everything has gone wrong, from the first sketched designs through cutting and finishing. The wood was knotty, the plane was dull, the bandsaw didn't cut right, there isn't enough space to work, I made a mistake cutting a mortise, and so on. If there was a chance for things to go wrong, they went wrong in a big way.

At such times, I usually stop work, switch off the power, and have a chat with one of my many woodworking buddies. And then when I start over, my mind is refreshed, I know a little more, and it all comes up roses. I instantly see how the mortise can be repaired, the plane cuts just right, I see that the bandsaw guide needs readjusting. And so it is with all woodworkers. When every step seems to be a sorry stumble, you can't do better than to seek advice.

This book involves sharing with you some of the woody wisdom I have picked up over the years—some of the make-it-all-right-in-the-end tips I know for sure will work. These pages are about the amazing feeling of achievement when, after a long struggle, a project works out. In many ways, it's the struggle and the sharing of knowledge that makes it all worthwhile.

Yes, of course, it's great when a project runs smoothly the first time through, but there is a lot of pleasure to be gained when a seemingly doomed project can be turned around at the eleventh hour. If you are a woodworker, then you know what I

ABOVE A contemporary writing desk, beautifully constructed from solid American cherry and maple by designer/craftsman Neil Clarke. Most cabinetmaking requires accuracy, ingenuity and a good knowledge of construction. Traditionally, if a cabinetmaker made a mistake, they usually had a way to remedy it.

ABOVE A chair designed in 1947 by Hans J. Wegner. Although mass-produced, the quality of workmanship and attention to detail is greater than in most hand-crafted work. The shaping and jointing is complex and subtle. To make this in a small workshop would require a lot of problem-solving techniques and jigs.

mean—one moment a project is a mess, and the next moment, after a talk with a friend in the know, a piece of innovative sleight-of-hand magic puts it back together. For my part, I find that not only do these rescued-from-the-brink projects give the most satisfaction, but they are often the most successful. It's almost as if the extra measure of sweat and effort and the comradeship and shared knowledge all come together to impart a special glow to the finished piece.

The fifty questions posed in this book come from an international survey of the most common problems that bug woodworkers. In answer to the fifty questions, our 200 plus solutions are a mix of traditional techniques we have gathered along the way, plus tips that have been passed on to us by other woodworkers. The intention of the book is to answer each of the questions with one or more solutions so that you can modify the answers to suit your own specific needs.

Alongside the text and the hands-on photographs, we have included working drawings, close-up illustrations, cross sections, computer imagery, and frequent cross-references—all to help you solve your woodworking problems. So, when a project goes wrong, don't panic and dump it in the wastewood barrel, but rather sit down quietly in your workshop, and leaf through the pages of our book. Best of luck!

How to use this book

Tinted panels make it easy to pick out the questions

Picture feature highlighting some of the things that can go wrong when you are woodworking

Each question has several possible solutions

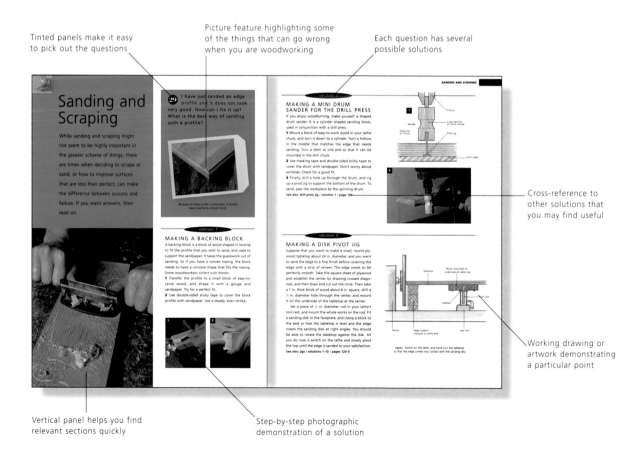

Cross-reference to other solutions that you may find useful

Working drawing or artwork demonstrating a particular point

Vertical panel helps you find relevant sections quickly

Step-by-step photographic demonstration of a solution

Workshop

Woodworking is a joyful activity, but only if your workshop is comfortable and well organized, with all your tools stored and arranged so they are close at hand. Be it ever so humble—a garage, shed or lean-to—if your workshop is dry, well-lit, clean and comfortable, then you, the wood and the tools are going to be as one.

1 My tools are scattered all over my workshop—how can I keep my tools organized and yet handy?

solution 1

STORING TOOLS ON PEGBOARDS

The traditional way to store tools is to buy one or more pegboards and wire clips that clip into the pegboard holes. These clips can be arranged in a pattern to hold your particular set of tools. If you want to create storage as a woodworking project, you can drill holes into boards and beams and glue dowels into them—or even whittle your own wooden pegs, and then hammer them into the holes you have drilled.

See also: drawknife / solution 1 / page 84,
whittling knife / solution 2 / page 85

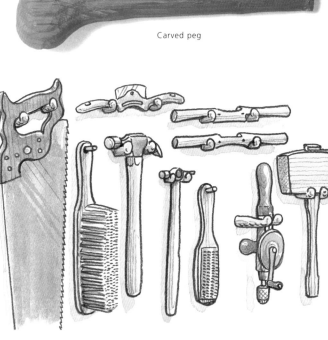

Carved peg

ABOVE Wooden pegs can easily be made from scrap pieces—we think they are a great idea!

solution 2

ABOVE A safe and accessible storage for power tools—note the lip that prevents them falling off the shelf.

SHELVES FOR POWER TOOLS

Power tools are best stored on shelves fixed about six inches below standing eye level. If you want to be a bit fancier, you can fasten a lip at the outer edge to prevent tools falling off, and tilt the shelves slightly to present the tools like exhibits. The tools should be on view and easy to reach.

See also: orderly working / solution 4 / page 13

solution 3

SHELVES FOR EDGED TOOLS

Chisels, gouges and planes need to be accessible and yet protected. Some woodworkers prefer to store chisels and gouges in slotted blocks and other edged tools in cupboards or on open shelves. I store all my chisels and gouges in cloth-lined compartments on shelves, so that each tool is in its own place and separated from its neighbors.

See also: chisels / solution 3 / page 47

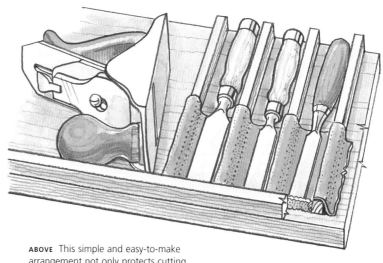

ABOVE This simple and easy-to-make arrangement not only protects cutting edges from damage, but also keeps tools in sight and easy to reach.

solution 4

FORSTNER BIT BLOCK

Forstner bits and router bits are more easily recognized by the shape of the head than by the number or size etched onto the shank, so they are best stored in drilled blocks. Select a length of wood thicker than the largest bit and about ½ in. wider

than the longest shank, plane it smooth, and then bore a pattern of holes in its edge, slightly larger than the shank diameter, and to a depth that allows each head of a bit to sit just clear of the block. Space the pattern of holes appropriately.

See also: drill press jig / solution 1 / page 120

RIGHT Traditional storage of drill bits in a block is still a good idea. The bits are protected from damage and you can see them at a glance.

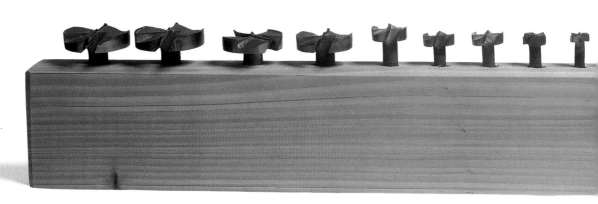

② My working environment is chaotic and inefficient—how can I organize my work procedures and steps?

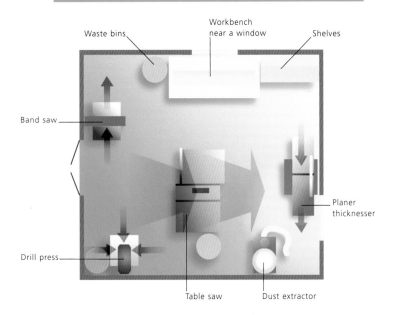

Waste bins

Workbench near a window

Shelves

Band saw

Planer thicknesser

Drill press

Table saw

Dust extractor

solution 1

AN ERGONOMIC LAYOUT

There is no such thing as the perfect workshop! No matter the size, you will want a flexible layout that can be adapted to your changing needs. Locate the floor-mounted tools and work surfaces with usable space around them. Consider the type of work that you produce and the large power tools you have, and design the layout accordingly. Think through a typical project—you take wood from its storage place, saw it to rough size, plane it, measure the pieces, use hand tools on it at the bench, and so on. Arrange your equipment so as to cut down on the walking, reaching and heavy lifting. Arrange the large tools and work surfaces so that you can move freely from one to the other, and so that all your hand tools are out of harm's way and yet easy to reach.

See also: spray booth / solution 3 / page 95

tools and resources / solution 5 / page 20

LEFT Design the layout of your workshop so that you have adequate room to work around each machine. Bear in mind you may need to plane really long planks and convert full size boards

solution 2

PRACTICAL PROCEDURES

Every procedure in the workshop needs to be carefully thought through in terms of space, time and movement. For example, when you are planing at the bench, it's important that you be able to put your hands on all the tools and other items you are likely to need. The same is true of working at standing power tools. When you are using, say, the band saw, it's important that all the guides, Allen keys and other helpers associated with that activity are at hand. The best way of organizing your setup is to take a project through all the procedures, and then arrange the storage and access to suit. For example, if you are working at the scroll saw and you find that the spare blades are out of reach, or that you have to reach over the saw table, or you need to walk across the shop to see the working drawings, then stop for a while and spend time rearranging things.

See also: table-saw push plane / solution 7 / page 124

solution 3

COMFORTABLE CONDITIONS

You, your wood and your tools all need the same environment. Your workshop needs to be dry, well lit with a balance of natural and artificial light, and at a temperature you consider to be comfortable. I have two workshops—a garden workshop that is 20 x 7 ft, and a garage shop that is 20 x 10 ft. The garden workshop has windows all along one long side, a bench and a work surface under the window, a door at each end, several flex lights that can be arranged to eliminate shadows, plenty of electrical outlets, small electric convection heaters, chests that contain my hand tools—and an old armchair. To my way of thinking, comfort equals efficiency. The garage workshop contains my lathe, a portable planer and a vacuum dust collector. The idea is that noise, dust and debris are confined to the garage workshop, while the more pleasurable hand-tool work is done in the garden workshop.

See also: saw horse table / solution 3 / page 86

solution 4

ORDERLY USE OF TOOLS

We are all sometimes tempted to rush through a project, using one tool after another, putting each down on the bench, and then going on to the next task. This approach is a no-no on many counts. The tools bang against each other and lose their cutting edges, the small tools are lost under piles of shavings and of course, the work surface soon gets to be so cluttered that you can no longer function efficiently. It is best to work at a controlled pace, and to get into the habit of putting tools back after using them. It's not a very exciting solution, but it works!

See also: racks / solution 2 / page 11

ABOVE A bench covered in tools is a bad idea—tool edges are damaged, tools are lost or mislaid, and there is no room to work.

solution 5

USING POWER TOOLS

While power tools—meaning everything from hand-held drills and routers to larger floor tools like band saws and planers—do definitely ease the way by taking some of the time-consuming labor out of the bigger jobs, it is vital for maximum efficiency and for safety's sake that they be routinely cleaned and regularly adjusted. You should spend time at the end of every working session cleaning up the dust and debris. First switch off the power, then sweep up the accumulation of shavings and sawdust that gathers around the base, wipe the surfaces with a cloth, and make sure that the nooks and crannies in and around the tool are clean. Pay particular attention to the air vents in the various motors. If you are not going to use a particular large tool for a time, it's a good idea to cover it with a dustcloth. I know of one woodworker who drapes large oil-dampened cloths over his floor tools—the cloths don't look great, but they keep the metal surfaces in good condition!

See also: power tool maintenance /

solution 1–10 / pages 112–15

RIGHT Dust and debris around the band saw blade may skew the workpiece.

solution 6

PERSONAL SAFETY

Assuming that you have fire extinguishers and smoke alarms, and that you periodically test your electrical circuits and connections, one of the worst health hazards in a woodshop is wood dust! To protect yourself, you can use hand tools that make shavings rather than dust, you can use dust collectors, and you can wear a mask. I favor using a full-face respirator mask when I am creating wood dust.

RIGHT If you are working with power tools, a good sized vacuum cleaner is a must. Get the largest and most powerful that money and space allows.

solution 7

GOOD LABELING

All chemical product containers must have good, clear labels! This is important if you transfer oil, varnish, glue or whatever from large containers into small jars and bottles. Use a permanent marker pen to write the contents and the use-by dates on the label. For safety's sake, do not store toxic substances in jars and bottles that once held food or drink—especially if you have small and curious children. If you must use them, then at least strip off the old labels and re-label.

See also: bleach / solution 1 / page 100

Timber

The pain and the pleasure of woodworking is the fact that a piece of lumber is unknown until it is sawed and planed. It might then reveal anything from a bad flaw to a grain pattern that is uniquely beautiful. The best you can do is cut the risks by learning as much as you can about the inherent qualities of wood. Here we show you the way.

3 I've been buying my wood at at a do-it-yourself home supply store. It is expensive and of not very good quality. Where is the best place to find good lumber for woodworking?

solution 1

FINDING SOURCES OF WOOD

The last place to go for quality timber is a general do-it-yourself store—the lumber they sell is usually construction grade, and not very good even for that. Better to search out a local woodworker's store that specializes in stocking such wood, or find a good lumberyard. The people there not only tend to have a good deal of expertise, but they are usually seeking to form long-lasting customer relationships. They have a personal interest in selling you top-quality wood. Pick a moment when they are not too busy, and tell them your needs. If they look bored and/or try to sell you unsuitable wood, go elsewhere.

See also: checking wood / solution 1 / page 36

solution 2

VISITING A LUMBERYARD

When you have drawn up your design, and made a specific board-by-board cutting list, and have decided what you need—the species of wood, the thickness, how seasoned it needs to be, the type of cuts you are after, and the like—it is time to visit the lumberyard. Put on work clothes and work shoes, and arm yourself with your list and a tape measure. Tell them what you need, ask them if you can look around, and then be prepared to spend time inspecting. Don't be afraid to crawl over the wood and to be picky, but bear in mind that yards and mills are potentially dangerous places. Once you have found what you want, ask how long it has been seasoned, check it over for problems, and ask questions. Don't forget, knowledge is power! The more you know, and the more they think you know, the better the deal.

See also: checking wood / solution 1 / page 36

irregular edges / solution 1 / page 16

CALCULATING LUMBER VOLUME

Most hardwood lumber is priced by the cubic foot, a block 12 x 12 x 12 in., or by the board foot, a 12 x 12 in. slab 1 in. thick. The best way to visualize a cubic foot of wood is to divide it up in your mind into 12 board-foot pieces, and then set them end to end/edge to edge to make up a board. You might go for a board 12 in. wide and 12 ft long. Or 24 in. wide and 6 ft long, and so on. If you make the slabs thinner, you get a longer board, and conversely if you make the slabs thicker, you get a shorter board. When you are calculating the cost of a project, the first thing you must figure out is how thick you want the various parts to be.

See also: dimensions /

solution 1 & 2 / page 22

RIGHT A cubic foot of wood shown as a 12 x 12 x 12 in. cube, divided into 12 slices 1 in. thick.

NEGOTIATING A PRICE

Many woodworkers are a bit intimidated when it comes to negotiating a price! They arrive at the sawmill or lumberyard and go for the first price that's mentioned. The thing you have to understand is that there are very few rules, other than that the yard owner is looking for the highest price! The best way is to ask for the unit price (per cubic or board foot), and then negotiate down. Let's say that you are looking for a 2-in. thick slab of lime about 12 in. wide and 6 ft long, and the yard is asking for $30 a cubic foot. They will realize that you have to allow for imperfect edges, splits at the end of a board, badly placed knots, sticker stains and all the rest. The moment that you see your board, you have to figure out in your mind just how you are going to work with it. Ask yourself—should you cut the defects away? Or are you going to work around them? At this point, you have to start haggling for a lower price—it's all part of the game.

See also: knots / solution 3 / page 17

sticker stains / solution 2 / page 16

ABOVE A stickered pile of wood arranged for air-drying. Note how the sticks are arranged more or less one above the other.

ABOVE A lot of these boards have split down the length. They can only be used for narrow components–you may be able to buy them cheaper.

4 I have just bought some bargain-priced wood, but there are many problems with it—irregular edges, stains, knots and so forth. Are there ways to use this wood to make good-looking projects?

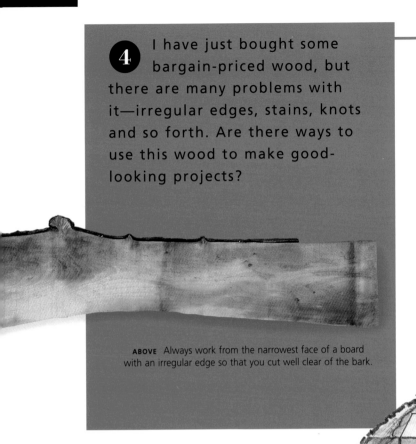

ABOVE Always work from the narrowest face of a board with an irregular edge so that you cut well clear of the bark.

solution 1

MAKING THE MOST OF THE WOOD

Though irregular edges do have to be cut back, don't make the mistake of always starting out by cutting a board back to a single end-to-end straight edge. It is much better to consider how you might divide up the board so the parts of the project can be obtained in ways that will minimize scrap. Especially if the wood is rare and expensive, the best procedure is to cut full-size patterns for all the parts, lay them out on the board, and then rearrange them until you have found a way to use most of the sound wood.

See also: lumber yard / solution 2 / page 14

LEFT Spend time working out how you can cut up a board most efficiently. If need be, arrange the short pieces so that they fit within the widest part of the board.

solution 2

ABOVE Use a scraper to remove the worst of the sticker stain.

REMOVING STICKER STAINS

While it is difficult to generalize about sticker stains—because so much depends upon the type of wood and the depth of the stain—the best way to start is by deciding how much of the stained face you can afford to cut back at the planing stage. Study the position of the stain in relationship to how the board is going to be cut, and how it fits into your project. Try to lay out the design so the stain is out of view—inside a cupboard, underneath the seat of a chair, inside a joint, and so on. After you run the wood through the planer and cut back as much as possible of the stained face, you will, if you are lucky, be left with only the shadow of a stain. Finally, take your scraper and spend time cutting back the area in and around the stain. If needs be, and the design allows, scrape the stained area slightly deeper than the surrounding wood.

See also: sticker stains / solution 4 / page 15

cabinet scraper / solution 5 / page 43

solution 3

PLUGGING A DEAD KNOT

1 Establish the extent of the knot, and decide on the shape and size of the plug. Select a piece of wood to match the grain, and cut the plug so that it covers the whole defective area around the knot.

2 Set the plug over the knot and scribe the board around the edge of the plug.

3 Cut the scrap from the board with a chisel.

4 Finally, glue the plug in place and smooth the surface with a plane.

See also: negotiating / solution 4 / page 15

solution 4

USING PROBLEM WOOD

When the time comes to begin a project, and you don't have enough good wood, so that you have to use a board that has serious imperfections, the best way to proceed is to consider how you can position the flaws so they are hidden from view. For example, you might use the board at the back or top of a cabinet, or under a seat, and so on. Another choice is to split a good board and the imperfect board, and glue the halves together so the fault is out of sight. Consider these kinds of problems at the beginning of a project and select your wood accordingly.

See also: laminating / solution 2 / page 27

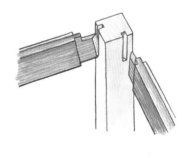

ABOVE
Use blemished wood in areas of a piece that will remain hidden from view—at bottom, back and under drawers.

ABOVE RIGHT AND RIGHT You can use blemished wood to back up good pieces, as shown with this table apron. Traditionally, second-choice boards are used at the backs of dressers and cabinets.

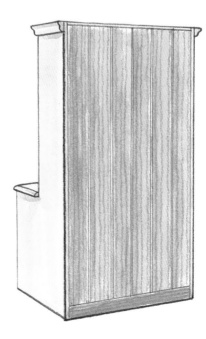

Planning

The successful project happens in your mind's eye and on the drawing board before you ever put tools to wood. If you spend time at the planning stage, and are painstaking in laying out, marking, figuring order of assembly, and so on, success will most surely follow. We here offer a few good, tested solutions.

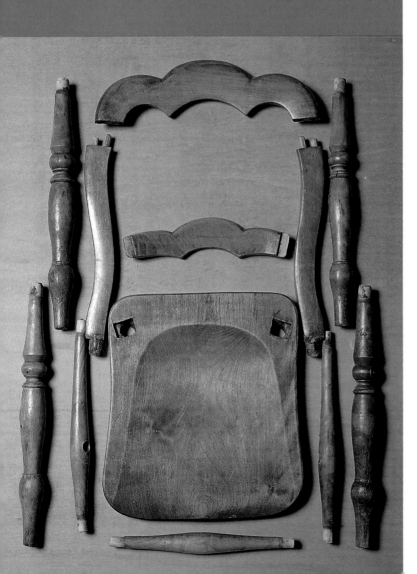

5 I am in trouble with my current project. There appears to be too many pieces of wood. How can I bring it to order?

solution 1

ABOVE The secret of a successful project is to familiarize yourself with the way the piece is constructed and put together. Spend time sketching out the joints and the order of work.

UNDERSTANDING CONSTRUCTION

First things first. Before you put tools to wood, familiarize yourself with the way the project should be cut and put together. Draw up plans, make sketches and a cut list—even use a computer to create a graphic of the project in the round if you have that capability. Continue until you have a clear picture in your mind's eye of the total project. Of course much depends upon the project, but if it is really complex, it is worthwhile building a scale model. If it is a truly special project—meaning it might bring you in more business, or it is prestigious, or it is going to use costly and rare wood, or you are building it for your mother and father's anniversary—then the only sure-fire way of getting a real grip on it is first to build a full-size version in inexpensive, easy-to-work softwood.

See also: mock-up / solution 1 / page 22

ACCURATE LAYING OUT

One of the primary ways of ensuring smooth progress through a project is to spend time at the layout stage making sure that every piece of material is correctly marked, named and numbered with the names and symbols connecting it to your plans and sketches. Start by drawing the cutting arrangement on a scrap of plywood and adding up the measurements. Try to group the parts so that you can rip through from end to end without cross-cutting. After making sure that all the parts are going to fit your chosen material, take a soft pencil, a ruler, a square and a straightedge, and mark out the project with all the parts that make up the design. Allow for subsequent sawing and planing by adding about ¾ in. to the length, ¼ in. to the width and ⅛ in. to the thickness of each part. Arrange the parts on the wood so that side-by-side pieces share the same cutting line where possible. If you are short of wood, reduce the allowance for scrap. When you have drawn all the parts on the face of the wood, checked and double checked that they are all there and correct, and made absolutely sure they are arranged so that the grain is running in the right direction, then label and number them.

See also: using story sticks / solution 2 / page 22

USING CLEAR SYMBOLS

Some projects are made up of dozens of parts, so it is vital that your symbols be clear and unambiguous. I use face-edge marks to identify the true face and edge, and triangle markings to show how groups of parts relate to each other. If mating parts are placed in the same order as they are when assembled, you can assume that the triangle always points up or away. If the parts are mixed up, you simply rebuild the triangle for the correct order.

See also: mock-ups / solution 1 / page 22

RIGHT It's important that each part of a piece carry two lines of the triangle—in this instance each board that makes up the slab.

RIGHT With this project, the woodworker has carefully considered the grain of the various boards and arranged them accordingly. Note that the two bottom drawer fronts are made from the same board.

CUTTING ORDER

After you have laid out on the roughly sawn boards with all the parts that go to make up the project, stop for a while and decide how best to cut each board. If you have spent time at the layout stage grouping pieces of the same length, and aligning those of the same width so that they run end to end through the wood, you should be able for the most part to rip through the board. Start by ripping as much as possible and then follow through with primary crosscutting. When you reach the point where you have a number of ripped parts, and a number of parts that you have crosscut away from the main body of the wood, then go back to using the rip saw to cut apart the grouped parts. The secret of success is always to assume that you are going to be short of wood, and to minimize scrap accordingly.

See also: assembly order / solution 6 / page 20

solution 5

CORRECT TOOLS AND RESOURCES

Before you take on a job, you need to sit down and consider all the implications. Ask yourself: Is your workshop big enough? Is there enough power? Are the machines big enough? Are the work surfaces large enough? Do you have enough clamps? Do you need more sawhorses? Do you need help picking up the wood and delivering the finished piece? Are your skills up to the task? Are there any techniques that you don't quite understand? Do you have enough money to buy the materials? Is it possible to cut costs by making some of the parts from cheaper wood? Is the hardware available? Do you need to redesign any of the parts to suit your tools? Do you need help at the assembly stage? And so on. Spend time figuring out the answers —then modify the project to suit your needs.

See also: workshop / solution 2 / page 12

LEFT For a project this complex, you need access to a good-sized lathe, plus a steamer, a former for the back bow, and a good knowledge of steam-bending.

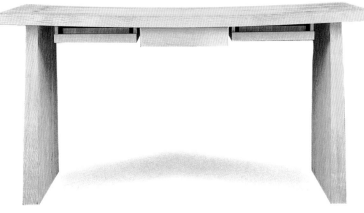

BELOW While this project may look simple and easy to make, you should bear in mind that its size alone dictates plenty of workshop space and a helping hand.

ABOVE LEFT For this box, each and every one of the hundred or so parts is cut to fit. More than anything else, it is a test of organizational skill, with each piece labeled so its place in the scheme of things is easy to identify.

solution 6

TRIAL ASSEMBLY

Once you have finished cutting all the pieces and making the various joints of the project and planing the surfaces, then comes the task of assembling the project. The best way is to undertake a dry run or glueless assembly—meaning you do everything except actually apply the glue. You clear space, set out the clamps and the glue, have cloths at the ready, and then put the project together and clamp it. What happens, of course, is that the dry run points up potential problems. So if you need more clamps, or more clamping blocks, or you need to ease a joint, or such and such a piece isn't quite right, then you get a chance to redo it. The risky way to go about this is to apply the glue, assemble, and then find that there are problems!

See also: gluing up / solution 3 / page 83

cutting order / solution 4 / page 19

LEFT A cabinet of this size requires great care and attention when gluing together. It is absolutely essential that the work area is completely level and smooth. The position of the clamps is also critical.

6 I have just started doing woodworking full time. I have a working drawing—how do I verify the dimensions before I start cutting?

BELOW Working drawing showing the back of a chair.

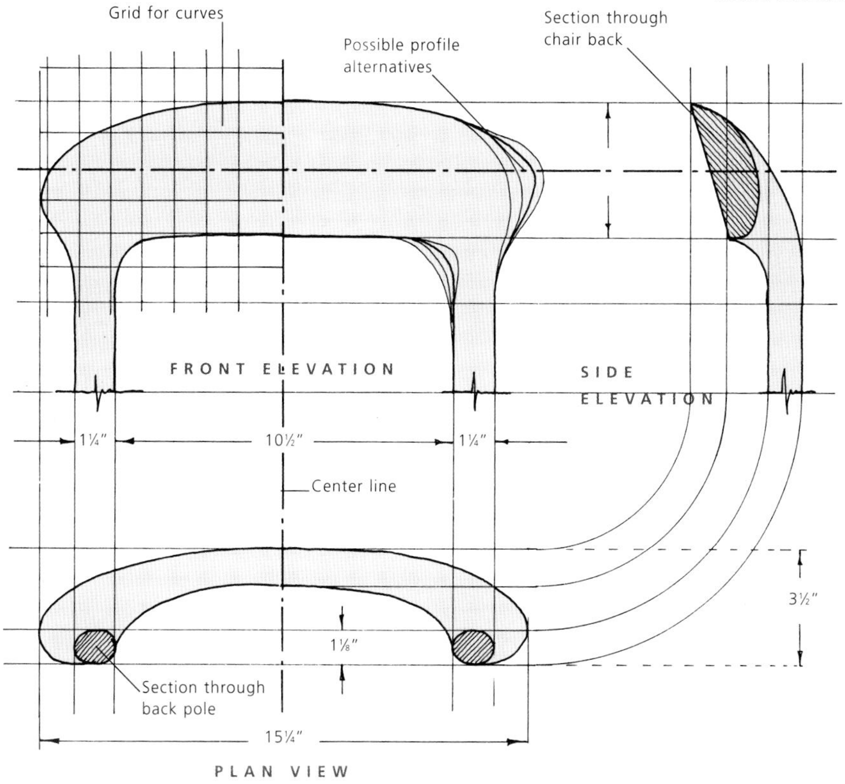
Grid for curves
Possible profile alternatives
Section through chair back
FRONT ELEVATION
SIDE ELEVATION
1¼"
10½"
1¼"
Center line
3½"
1⅛"
Section through back pole
15¼"
PLAN VIEW

solution 1

CALCULATING DIMENSIONS

The very first thing to do when you are presented with a working drawing is to look for dimensions. Most commonly, they are stated in fractions of inches, inches and feet, and written on the drawing between arrowheads. Or dimensions are given in metric form: millimeters, centimeters and meters. Some drawings are done to scale, meaning that, for example, ¼ in. on the drawing equals 1 ft, and you must measure the dimensions and translate them to full size. Or the drawing may be done on a grid, with a scale that reads "one grid square is 1 inch square." Again, you must translate the grid to dimensions of each part so that you will know how to measure and cut.

See also: calculations / solution 3 / page 15, chair legs / solution 6 / page 77

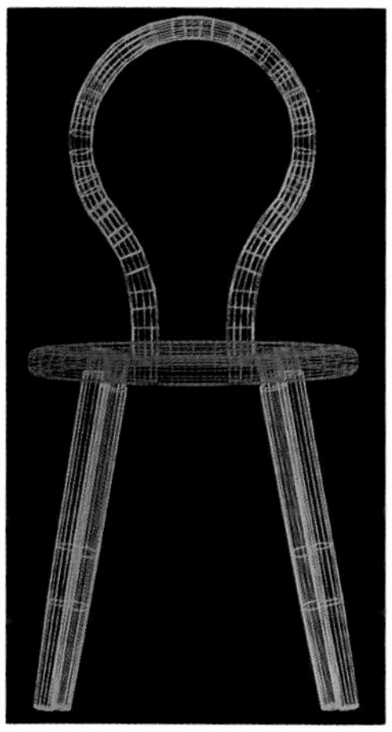

LEFT A three-dimensional computer model of a chair. Front, side, plan and auxillary views can be printed out full size from such a model.

solution 2

CONVERSION PROBLEMS

Some working drawings give both metric and English measurements, or mix them together. The problem is that it's easy to get confused. You think you are reading inches, but it is a metric measurement, and you cut a piece to the wrong size. The best way to deal with this risk is to choose one standard, and then take a pen and white-out and go through the drawings, deleting or translating and re-marking all the measurements given in the other standard.

See also: lumber / solution 3 / page 15

METRIC EQUIVALENCY CHART

inches	mm	inches	mm	inches	mm
⅛	3	4½	114	20	508
¼	6	5	127	21	533
⅜	10	6	152	22	559
½	13	7	178	23	584
⅝	16	8	203	24	610
¾	19	9	229	25	635
⅞	22	10	254	26	660
1	25	11	279	27	686
1¼	32	12	305	28	711
1½	38	13	330	29	737
1¾	44	14	356	30	762
2	51	15	381	31	787
2½	64	16	406	32	813
3	76	17	432	33	838
3½	89	18	457	34	864
4	102	19	483	35	889

Design, Layout and Fitting

When, as a child, I asked my grandfather how he intended to do a certain project, he would wink and say knowingly—"There are ways, there are ways, and there are ways; why don't you stay and learn something!" He was right—I always knew the answers at the end.

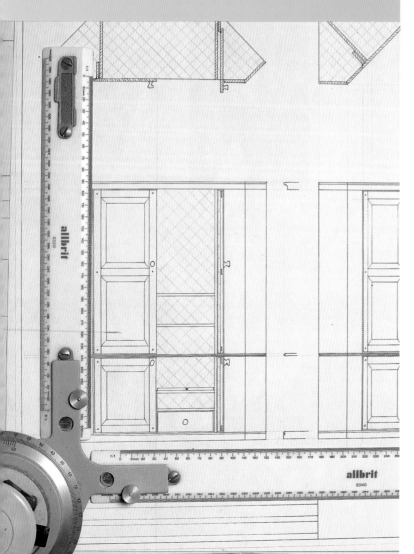

7 My poor math skills are getting in the way of my woodworking. Is there a way of laying out a project that minimizes the need for rules and calculators?

STORY STICKS AND RODS

A story stick or pole is a clean piece of wood that is laid out with all the full size dimensions and details that go to make up the design of a piece of furniture. The system dates back to the time before paper was commonplace and when cabinetmakers were perhaps illiterate. Joiners, chairmakers and framers still use poles to transfer measurements. The pole is either set out from a working drawing, or directly from a piece of furniture that you want to duplicate. Though rods are in many ways the same as story sticks, the term has come to mean full size mock-ups that are made in flat sheet material—more like a working model or prototype. So, for example, a chair might be mocked up in plywood—so that you can test out its proportions.

See also: construction / solution 1 / page 18

solution 2

USING STORY STICKS

The wonderful thing about story sticks and rods, is that the whole system works without the need for measurements and calculators. Let's say then, that a client wants you to copy a Hope chest in a museum. All you do, is sketch the chest, and then set the story sticks against the piece and pencil off the various widths and heights direct. Ideally you need three sticks, one for the vertical height, one for the width across the front, and one for the depth. And of course, if there are unusual joints, or fancy details or whatever, then these are all written down on the stick. All necessary details and notes are written down. When you get back to the workshop, you then set the sticks down alongside your chosen wood and either copy the measurements off direct, or step them off with a pair of dividers.

See also: laying out / solution 2 / page 19

solution 1

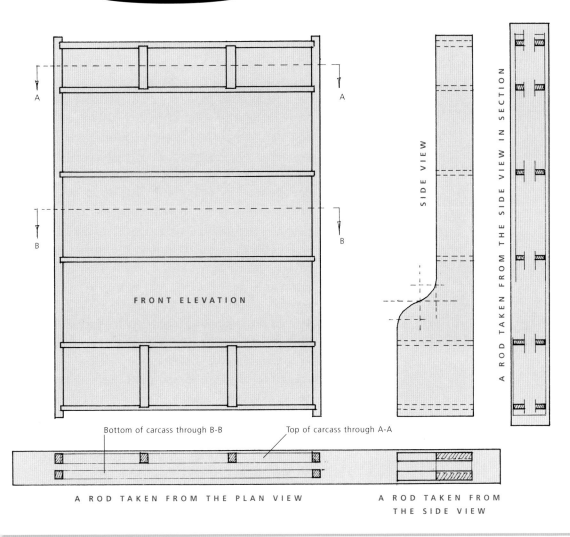

FRONT ELEVATION

SIDE VIEW

A ROD TAKEN FROM THE SIDE VIEW IN SECTION

Bottom of carcass through B-B

Top of carcass through A-A

A ROD TAKEN FROM THE PLAN VIEW

A ROD TAKEN FROM THE SIDE VIEW

LEFT A working drawing of the front and side elevations of a cabinet. For the drawing to be of any use in the workshop, it must be actual size and preferably drawn on to a sheet of hardboard (which can be painted white to show the lines better). For convenience, the critical dimensions can then be marked on to smaller pieces of board or even sticks. A good way to check dimensions before you start cutting is to lay your piece of wood over the drawing itself.

ABOVE Set the story stick directly against the piece and transfer the measurements of the various component parts.

ABOVE Set the story stick alongside your chosen piece of wood and transfer the measurements.

8 I have just finished making a custom cabinet—it turned out perfectly! Unfortunately it won't fit flush to the wall, because the wall is uneven and the baseboard gets in the way. What can I do?

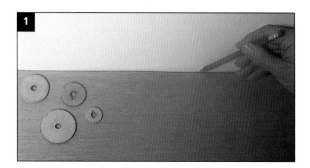

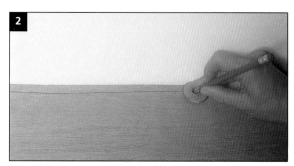

solution 1

SCRIBING WHEEL

Traditionally, scribing or coping is a technique by which one piece is cut and shaped to fit over another—as in marking and cutting the corner miter on a baseboard. Some woodworkers now use the terms to describe ways of shaping one piece to fit against another. One such technique, known as "wheel scribing," is used to mark the curve when the edge of a panel or board must fit flush with an uneven wall. In action, a small wooden wheel is drilled with a center hole for a pencil point, the board to be marked is set against the uneven wall, and the pencil point drawn down the board with the wheel against the wall. The wheel is easily made from scrap plywood—it's a trick that works every time!

1 Place the cabinet against the wall and slide the loose-fit surface board up against the wall but square with the front of the cabinet frame. Move it around for the best fit and work out how big the gap is. Clamp the board in place so that it stays put.

2 Select a wheel of the right size, and place it over the point of a sharpened soft pencil. Put the wheel on the surface so that its edge is butted up against the wall. Now, with your index finger pressing down on the wheel so that it doesn't ride up, and all along the way making sure the edge of the wheel stays in contact with the wall, drag the wheel along so that the pencil makes its mark. If you get it right, the line will perfectly follow the shape of the wall.

3 When you are confident that the line is where you want it, cut away the scrap from the edge of the board with a fine-toothed saw—a coping saw, scroll saw, compass saw, or even a bow saw. I have used a saber saw.

4 Finally, after you have sanded the edge to a smooth surface, reclamp the board onto the cabinet frame and slide it back in place against the uneven wall. If you got it right, it will be a beautiful flush fit.

See also: cutting curves / solution 9 / page 115

solution 2

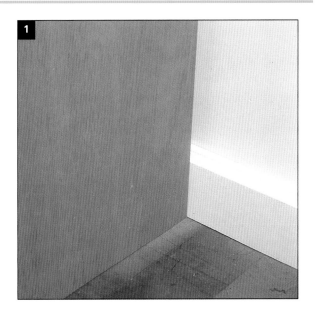

ABOVE The profile gauge gives two readings, a positive and a negative. With this, you can cut an identical profile or a mating piece.

PROFILE GAUGE

The profile gauge or shape tracer is a small hand-sized tool used to copy a shape and act as a template. In use, a row of steel needles is pushed against a complex shape to record it. It's the perfect tool for copying such shapes as door or baseboard moldings.

1 Start by pushing the gauge against the floor so that all the needles are aligned. Push until the greater length of the needles is on one side of the central bar. Then place the gauge against the baseboard so that it is at right angles to the wall, and push it firmly towards the wall, so that the needles slide back and follow the shape of the irregular profile of the baseboard. Stop when the leading needles are up against the wall.

2 Lay the gauge down flat on the board so that it is aligned correctly, and then use a soft pencil to trace the shape of the needles. Remove the gauge and smooth up the profile.

3 Finally, first make sure that you haven't copied the wrong part of the profile, and then take a small fine-toothed hand saw, say a coping saw or a fret saw, and very carefully cut the cabinet board—on the scrap side of the line that you drew.

See also: cutting curves / solution 9 / page 115

mitered joints / solution 2 / page 64

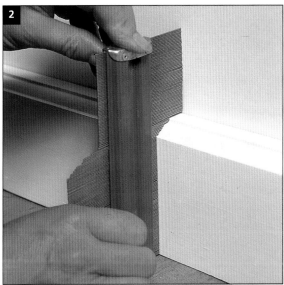

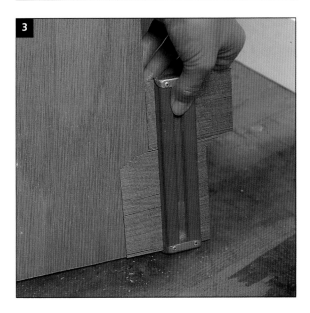

9 I have managed to get some good wood at a good price, but it is too thin. I have a project that requires thicker stock. Can you come up with a good laminating design to make wood thicker?

INTERLOCKING JOINT

This particular right-angled corner joint not only laminates stacks of thin-section wood with a minimum of layout and fancy cutting, but better yet, it is rigid, strong and attractive. It's a beauty—a bit like a Chinese puzzle—but easy when you know how!

1 Assuming that your wood is ¾ in. thick and has true faces, edges and ends, set the mortise gauge points to ¾ in., with the fence set at ⅜ in., and mark out the width of the dado by running scribed lines across the width and down the edges. Do this on all six boards.

2 Set the marking gauge to ⅜ in. and establish the depth of the dado by scribing a line along the length of the grain so that it crosses the gauged lines. Shade in the scrap parts to avoid mistakes in cutting.

3 Cut the dado with a fine-toothed saw, and then use a bevel-edged chisel to pare out the scrap. Aim for a tight friction fit, ⅜ in. deep and ¾ in. wide.

4 Cut the end off one board so that you are left with a ¾ in. rabbet—and then do a trial assembly of all six boards. Draw in registration triangles so that you know what goes where, and then disassemble, glue, reassemble and clamp.

See also: corner clamp / solution 4 / page 76

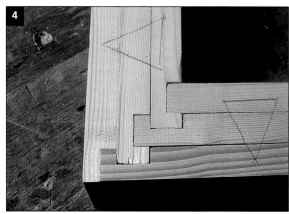

VENEER STRIP LAMINATING

When you are laminating pieces of thin wood to make larger sections, one way of making a positive design feature of a necessity is to sandwich strip veneers between the laminations. This technique is particularly useful when you are forced to use thin wood—it creates the illusion that the laminations were done for decorative reasons.

1 Plane all the mating faces of both the main pieces and the veneers, and then use a toothed plane or a toothed scraper to roughen the surface. Spread glue over all mating surfaces and clamp. Set the clamps every 6 in. or so along the workpiece.

2 When the glue is fully dry, plane the edges down to the level of the laminations, and use the resulting sections in the way you intended to use the thick wood.

See also: problem wood / solution 4 / page 17

laminating / solution 2 / page 45

ABOVE The size and arrangement of the veneers and the laminations is your personal choice.

ABOVE Veneer strips can be used as a decoration, to emphasize rather than hide the laminations.

10 I have built a small chest. I don't think brass hinges look right on it. I would like to use wooden hinges. Is it too late at this stage? Can you come up with a couple of designs?

RIGHT The dovetail hinge is a clever idea—one half of the hinge locks into the lid of the chest. It is functional and decorative.

INTEGRAL DOVETAIL HINGE

An integral dovetail hinge, set with the grain bridging the hinge, is an attractive solution that draws its inspiration from the butterfly key. It's relatively easy to attach and it's strong. Better yet, if you have damaged the edge of the lid installing the metal hinge, you may be able to position this hinge so that the damaged area is cut away.

1 Having drawn the shape of your hinge to size, put it in place so that it bridges the hinge board and the lid, and score around it with a knife. For a good fit, use a coping saw and a paring chisel to cut out the scrap.

2 When you have achieved a good friction fit, use a small plane to round the edge of the dovetail side of the hinge block and the edge of the hinge board. Aim for a half-roundnose profile.

3 With the hinge plate set in place, run a hole through the end of the hinge board and on through the hinge. The hole should run right through the hinge and out the other side.

4 When you have tested the fit and movement, glue the dowel and the dovetail.

See also: hinges / solution 1 / page 92

ABOVE The laminated surface hinge leaves the body of the chest intact, and it acts as a stop to prevent the lid from falling back.

LAMINATED SURFACE HINGE

If the design of your chest is such that you don't want to cut into the main body, and/or you want a hinge that has its own built-in stop, then this surface-mounted hinge is the answer.

1 Cut a plywood template and transfer the profile to the edge of a piece of straight-grained hardwood. You need six profiles for each hinge that you want to make.

2 Chuck a hole cutter in your drill, and then cut the dowel hole through all six profiles—but drill the saw hole on only three profiles, and to a depth of ¾ in.

3 Saw a ½ in. wide strip off the edge of the wood—holes and all. Spread out the six profiles, arrange them in order and trim them to fit. Spread glue on mating faces, slide a dry-fit dowel in place, and clamp.

4 Sand and trim the hinge to fit and then test its movement. When you have achieved a smooth action, glue the dowel pin in place.

5 Finally, set the hinge in place on the chest lid and screw it into place from underneath.

See also: laminating / solution 2 / page 89

Sawing

Sawing is a skill and can be a pleasure. If you select the right saw—and it is sharp—then there is nothing quite like the sound as it moves through the wood. But if you use the wrong saw for the wrong job, in the wrong way, the screeching as the saw does its mischief is simply dire. If you want to know how to do it right, keep on reading.

11 I am cutting four tenons. I have cut two already, and they are loose and sloppy. How can I make them tight and good-looking? And how can I cut good tenons the next time?

ABOVE A loose and sloppy joint is both structurally unsound and a pain to the eye.

solution 1

GLUING SHIMS

If you have a loose tenon that needs tightening up—meaning the tenon has been cut poorly, rather than the mortise, and you don't want to scrap it and start over—one of the easiest quick fixes is to shim it. The  procedure is simple. All you do is cut thin shims or wedges from the same wood as the tenon, dip them in glue, and tap them in on all four sides of the tenon until it's tight. Make sure that the joint is true, leave it until the glue is cured, and then plane and/or sand for a smooth surface. If there are gaps, use wood filler or filler glue as well as shims.

See also: tenons / solution 2 / page 46

using shims / solution 4 / page 81

gluing / solution 2 / page 75

ABOVE Cut the shims from the same wood as the workpiece, and tap them in on all four sides of the joint so that they go down to the level of the shoulder.

CORRECT USE OF THE MORTISE GAUGE

The most common mistake beginners make when they are working on mortise and tenon joints is that they do not set the marking gauge correctly, and then they make things worse by cutting on the wrong side of the marked lines. They finish up with a tenon that is too small and a mortise that is too large, both adding up to a loose joint.

1 Set the two points of the mortise gauge precisely on the corners of the chisel and tighten. Set the fence so that the pins are centered on your chosen piece of wood—so that they are on target from both sides of the wood. Do not try to set the gauge by knocking it on the bench.

2 Hold the workpiece steady—in the vise or tight to your body—and scribe the line with a dragging stroke. Use the same pin setting to scribe the mortise. Remember that when you cut the tenon, the saw must cut on the scrap side of the scribed line.

See also: cutting in / solution 3 / page 49

joints / solution 4 / page 32

CORRECT WAY TO MARK THE SHOULDER LINE

What most beginners fail to realize is that the fit of a tenon often depends on the width of the marking line at the shoulder and the position of the saw in relationship to that line. Tenon shoulders should be scribed with a knife, and the saw cut made to the scrap side of the line.

1 Take your piece of trued wood, and set the square against the mark. Butt the wooden stock up against the workpiece, and grip the stock and the workpiece together between your thumb and fingers. Do this on the bench—not in mid air! Hold the flat side of the knife against the blade and scribe a line with a dragging stroke.

2 Finally, set the workpiece in the vise, take a sharp paring chisel, tilt it slightly, and cut a narrow furrow to the scrap side of the scored line. The purpose of the furrow is to act as a guide for the saw blade.

See also: cutting / solution 2 / page 35

ABOVE A good joint is the perfect combination of form and function—a joy to the eye and structurally sound.

WAYS TO ACHIEVE GOOD JOINTS

Though there are just about as many ways to create a tight joint the first time as there are woodworkers, there are one or two rules of thumb that you can always count on. Certainly you can always take the time to repair a botched joint—and making good on bad work is perhaps half the pleasure for many woodworkers—but if you want to become a master, there are certain key procedures you must follow:

■ Use well-seasoned, top-quality, straight-grained wood, free from flaws like knots and splits.

■ Make sure that the wood has been trued on all faces, edges and ends.

■ Double-check your working drawings.

■ Be vigilant when you are laying out measurements—never take the readings for granted.

■ Make sure that your gauges and squares are accurate.

■ Make sure that your edged tools are sharp.

■ Choose your saws with care, and always use a fine-toothed blade.

■ Be painstaking at the gluing and clamping stage.

See also: joints / solution 2 / page 31

12 I am trying to cut out identical pieces with a scroll saw. The saw vibrates a great deal, so every piece I cut out is slightly different. How can I adjust the saw? How can I make sure all the pieces are identical?

INSTALLING AND ADJUSTING THE SAW

The electric scroll saw is without doubt one of the easiest machines to use—and this very fact all too often results in its being taken for granted and treated like a toy. Fledgling woodworkers just set their new scroll saw on the bench, switch it on and start sawing. The result is that it bounces around and ruins their work. The best arrangement is to bolt the saw onto its own dedicated table. This arrangement cuts out all vibration. Some woodworkers favor a long bench seat that they can sit on at one end, with the machine bolted down at the other end. Choose the correct blade and install it so that it is loose-pivoted at top and bottom. Adjust the tension so that the blade pings when it's plucked.

See also: cutting curves / solution 9 / page 115

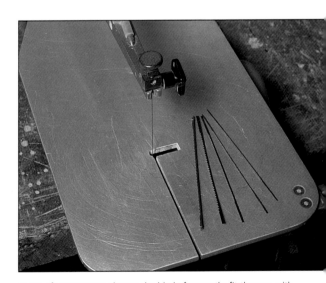

ABOVE If you want to change the blade frequently, fit the saw with easy-to-turn blade clamps, ones with big thumbscrews.

solution 2

SANDWICH CUTTING

Many woodworkers use the scroll saw for making small wooden items like toys with lots of identical parts. Let's say, for example, that you want to cut seven identical number shapes out of wood ⅛ in. thick, with each number standing about 3 in. high and 2 in. wide.

1 Cut seven wooden mats—one for each cutout that you want to make. Transfer the image to one mat and shade in the scrap areas. Sandwich the mats together with double-sided sticky tape so that the image is on top of the stack.

2 Fit the saw with a new fine-toothed blade so that the teeth point down, and adjust the tension until the blade pings. Wipe the work table with a cloth, and make sure that the saw is in good order. Hold the stack firmly down on the table and push it into the saw at a steady pace. Guide and maneuver the stack so that the moving blade is always presented with the next cutline. Don't force the pace and don't ease off the downward pressure of your hands.

3 When you have sawed around the image, ease the layers apart and remove the tape. If you have done things as described, the sawed edge will be so smooth that it hardly needs sanding.

See also: scroll saw / solution 4 / page 34

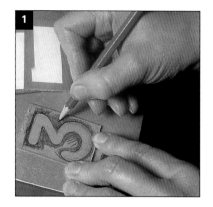

solution 3

CUTTING TIGHT ANGLES

A common problem that beginning woodworkers have when using the scroll saw is cutting tight angles correctly. They either go too slow and burn the wood, or they change direction too rapidly, which twists and breaks the blade. The rules below describe the right way.

■ If you want to keep the wood on both sides of the cutline, slow down at the angles and mark time so that the blade clears space around itself, and then change direction.

■ If the wood within the angle is scrap, run the blade straight through the middle of it to the angle, then back the blade out and make cuts from each side that follow the line and finish at the angle.

■ The finer the blade teeth and the tighter the tension, the easier it is to turn at an angle.

■ Don't try to turn at an angle with an old blade.

See also: scroll saw / solution 4 / page 34

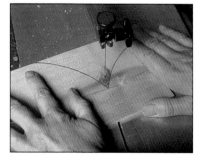

LEFT First cut straight through to the point of the angle, and then gently back out.

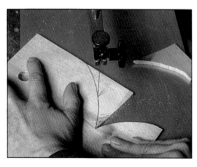

LEFT Make two follow-up cuts along the drawn lines so that the scrap comes away in two pieces.

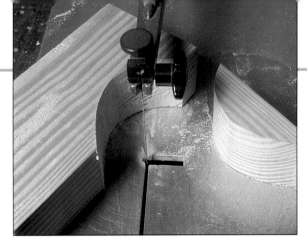

solution 4

CUTTING THICKER STOCK

There is no big secret to cutting thicker stock on the average scroll saw, other than that you must use a new, heavyweight coping saw type of blade set at correct tension. My particular saw can cut wood 1¾ in. thick. Of course, I do have to choose my wood with care and go slowly, but it can be done. Now I have discovered that there is a scroll saw on the market able to cut wood up to 4 in. thick!

See also scroll saw / solution 3 / page 33

ABOVE Always match blade and speed of feed to wood and depth of cut—the thicker the wood, the wider the blade and the slower the speed of advance.

13 I have just cut some wood to make a box. The ends of the pieces are rough and ragged. How can I fix them? How can I avoid doing this the next time?

ABOVE A ragged, close-to-the-line cut can be repaired!

solution 1

REMOVING THE SHARP EDGE

If you sawed your wood more or less to the finished length and the end cut is ragged, and there is no going back and starting over, then a good low-tech way to proceed is to plane off the ragged (arris) edge so that you finish up with a slightly mitered edge. Of course this doesn't work in all situations, but the miter does at least draw the eye away from the bad cut. What you do is clamp the workpiece in a vise, skew the plane to skim off the end, and then cock the block plane over at an angle and plane in from each edge. Make sure that the plane is razor sharp, otherwise you will have a ragged saw cut and a ragged miter!

See also: supporting blocks / solution 2 / page 40

tuning / solution 3 / page 41

LEFT The miter cuts away the ragged edge, and beguiles the viewer into believing that it is a positive design feature.

ABOVE Plane from side to middle to avoid splitting off the grain.

WAYS OF MAKING A BETTER CUT

A good part of achieving a smooth cut when you are cutting a small section of wood to length has to do with controlling the workpiece. Let's say that you are using a backsaw about 12 to 16 in. long with 12 to 14 points to the inch, and cutting a piece of 4 x ½ that is 13 in. long into 12 in. lengths. In this case, the bench hook is a pretty good option, because the ½ in. of waste at each end has very little weight and so can easily be cut away without the need for support. Then again, let's say that you want to cut the 12 in. lengths from a piece 6½ ft long, then the best way is to use a sizing board. All you do is clamp the board in the vise, set the stop at 12 in., slide your wood up against the stop, set the saw into the slot and make the cut. The good thing about using the sizing board is that the wood is fully supported on both sides of the cut.

See also: shoulder line / solution 3 / page 31

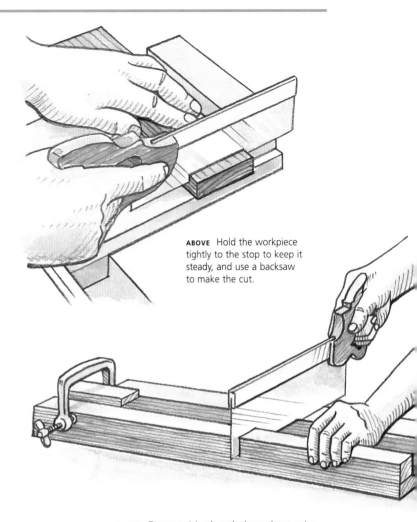

ABOVE Hold the workpiece tightly to the stop to keep it steady, and use a backsaw to make the cut.

ABOVE To use a sizing board, clamp the stop in place and then butt the end of the wood against the stop to make the cut. This is a good setup for cutting many identical pieces.

ABOVE If you are using a table saw for a close-to-the-line cut, be sure to slide a scrap piece under the workpiece to bear the brunt of any blade-exit splitting.

RIGHT No matter the tool—handsaw or power saw—and no matter if the wood has been resawn or cut across the grain, the workpiece will invariably need to be reworked with a hand plane. This being so, it is always a good idea to allow for subsequent planing by cutting slightly to the scrap side of the drawn line.

Planing

Hand planes and power planers/jointers are essential tools for creating flat, smooth surfaces or dressing edges on wood, but more can go wrong when using them than in any other woodworking procedure. If you have trouble getting the results you want with your planes or planers, then the following discussion will help you improve your work.

14 My planer is cutting a rough surface. What is the best method of planing a piece of wood to avoid a rough-looking finish?

ABOVE If the planer chews and chomps its way through wood, then you need to pinpoint the problem by looking at all aspects of the planing operation: everything from the type of wood to the workings of the parts of the plane.

CHECK OUT THE WOOD

Successful planing or jointing starts with the wood. Never buy lumber sight unseen. When you have decided the dimensions and number of pieces you want, write down a complete list of them. If there are minimum dimensions—meaning it can be bigger, but it can't be smaller—or you would be prepared to take Japanese cherry if they can't manage the English, then write it all down. It's vital that you go fully armed with a list. Be warned: if you give the impression that you are prepared to accept something less than perfect, then the chances are you will get it. Go to a woodworker's store or lumberyard and see what they have to offer. Begin by checking the color and grain. Look for clear wood with a good grain pattern, and without knots, cracks or end splits. Avoid warped boards and stained boards, or boards that show signs of fungus and mildew. Spend time looking through the wood pile—don't be rushed. Check the boards on both faces. Take into account end scrap and side scrap. Make sure that your choice is right for you.

See also: lumber / solution 2 / page 14

featherboard jig / solution 8 / page 124

LEFT This piece of wood is faulty on at least two counts: it is stained, and it shows knots that have soft, spongy centers.

ABOVE A moisture meter will tell you all you need to know about the moisture content of wood.

LEFT This wood, badly split along the length of the grain, will fall apart when cut.

GAUGING MOISTURE CONTENT

It's critically important that the wood you use be well-seasoned. You can check the moisture content with a small hand-held meter. All you do is spike the wood so that the current runs parallel with the grain, and then take a reading. The meter should be able to read 10–28% moisture in graded steps. Not only is it important that you use well-seasoned wood, you may want to ask how it was dried. Some woodworkers believe that air-dried wood behaves better than kiln-dried wood. They say that air-dried wood—meaning wood that has been allowed to dry in the open air, not heat-dried in an oven—planes smoother, has a better color and is easier to work.

See also: moisture / solution 1 / page 66

humidity / solution 1 / page 64

LEFT Although this piece of wood looks good from one face and edge, it reveals a split when it is flipped over that renders it useless.

LEFT Don't use wood with a knot that runs from face through to edge, because it's likely to break out.

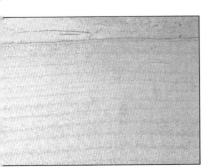

LEFT A piece of soft sappy wood will most certainly let you down.

ABOVE You simply spike this particular meter in the wood and turn the dial until the red light goes on.

SERVICING PLANER KNIVES AND TABLES

If your wood appears to be chewed on one side, and/or furrowed, it could be that the knives need resharpening or even replacing, or the table and/or knife settings are out of true. If you suspect that this might be the case, first run pieces of different types and various qualities of wood through the planer, to make sure that your wood isn't at fault. Then stop and read the user's manual. Once you have eliminated wood and user problems, and once you are aware of your particular tool's idiosyncrasies, switch it off and pull the plug. If there are other people in the workshop, tell them what you are doing. When the tool cannot be accidentally restarted, then you can begin the checks.

1 Take a good look at the wood and see if the roughness tells a story. For example, is the wood torn? The cutter knives may be blunt or you may have tried to plane against the grain. Is there a large step-up on the leading edge of the wood? The infeed table may be too low. Is the trailing end of the wood chewed? The infeed table may be set too high. Is the planed face furrowed along its length? The knives are chipped.

2 If the wood is furrowed along its length, chances are the knives are nicked. Study the planer so that you are absolutely familiar with its workings and the way it breaks down. Then carefully remove the cutterhead. If the knives are nicked, you need to get them resharpened. Some machines are fitted with double-edged throwaway knives. If this is the case, you can simply turn the knives around on their location studs, or attach new knives.

3 Once you have eliminated problems with the knives, the next step is to ensure that the tables are correctly set. As the takeoff or outfeed table is preset and tangential to the cutterhead, the problem usually has to do with the infeed table. With the cutterhead turned so that the knife is out of the way, place a metal straightedge from one table to the other, and make adjustments to the infeed table until it is set square or tangential to the cutterhead. Measure the distance between the edges of the two tables at both ends of the cutterhead space. Adjust the table until the edges are parallel.

See also: tuning planes / solution 1 / page 42

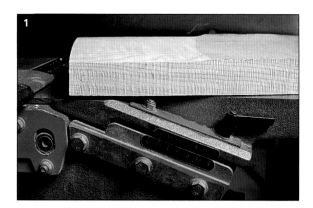

The 2-inch mark · Measuring rule · Outfeed table · Cutter block · Planer body · Cutters · 2

ABOVE You can set planer blades parallel and at the correct height by using a rule or a length of wood to measure the carryover distance of the blade.

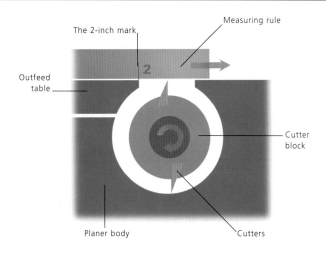

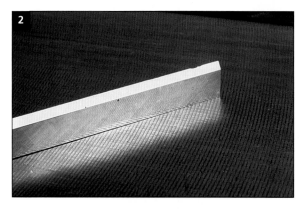

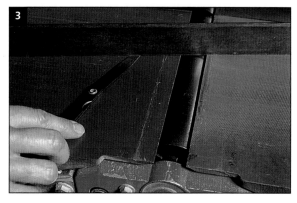

OVERALL ADJUSTMENTS

Give your planer a through examination from top to bottom, to make sure that every slot, screw, surface and shim is clean and correctly set. Start by switching off the power and pulling out the plug.

1 Check the fence with an engineer's square. If it is loose, or out of true, make adjustments until it is tight and at right angles to the tables. Replace any washers or nuts and bolts that are missing, worn or damaged.

2 After using a small brush and a vacuum cleaner to remove all the dust and debris, spend time removing the resin and grease. Wipe the surfaces with a clean cloth soaked in mineral spirits. If there are lumps or spatters of paint or resin, remove them with a wedge of hardwood. Don't use a metal tool; you'll scratch the working surfaces of the planer.

3 If the tool rattles, or the belts slap, or the cutterhead sometimes comes to a halt, it could be that the various belts and chains need overhauling. Remove the cover, and check the chain and the amount of slack in the belts. Make sure that the moving parts don't smack against the casing or the body of the tool or against each other.

See also: controlling feed / solution 1-3 / page 42

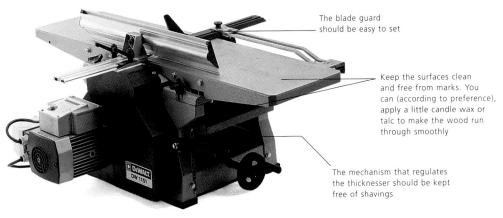

RIGHT One of the best ways of achieving a good planer cut is to familiarize yourself with every aspect of your particular planer. Study the manual and spend time making practice cuts.

The blade guard should be easy to set

Keep the surfaces clean and free from marks. You can (according to preference), apply a little candle wax or talc to make the wood run through smoothly

The mechanism that regulates the thicknesser should be kept free of shavings

15 I have just finished hand-planing a piece of end grain, and the grain split off! How do I fix it? And how do I avoid splitting end grain when planing?

ABOVE One of the worst things about splitting when planing end grain is the fact that it can so easily be avoided!

solution 1

GLUE REPAIR

I am always disgusted with myself for splitting an end grain when planing across it—because it is so easy to avoid! The good thing is that it can be corrected. You simply ease some glue into the split with a slip of paper and then clamp it or wrap it with masking tape. If the workpiece is special—a prestigious project or an irreplaceable piece of wood—then I use quick-setting glue to speed up the procedure. Glue the split as soon as it occurs—while the torn faces will still fit back together well. If a piece of wood has broken away or the wood is to be sanded, use a glue that is not gummy.

See also: gluing / solution 1 / page 78

glues / solution 1 / page 82

ABOVE Glue the split back together as soon as it occurs, before the sliver is lost or damaged.

solution 2

USING A SUPPORTING BLOCK

Using supporting blocks when planing across end grain is a simple procedure. All you do is clamp a block of scrap wood against the workpiece, so that the plane runs straight through and splits off a part of the scrap rather than the workpiece. Some woodworkers use scrap support blocks to plane with the grain as well as at the end. They claim that the additional side pieces not only prevent splitting off the long edges, but also that the greater width makes it easier to keep the block plane true to the face being worked.

See also: removing the arris / solution 1 / page 34

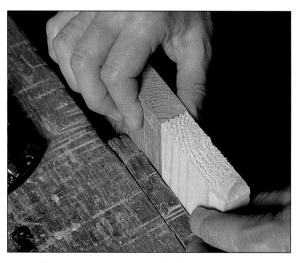

ABOVE Clamp a scrap piece to the side of the workpiece so that it receives the brunt of the cut as it runs out.

ABOVE Further minimize the risk of split-out by planing at an angle in order to shear the wood.

solution 3

ADJUSTING A BLOCK PLANE

Designed originally for trimming the end grain of butchers' blocks, the block plane is different from large bench planes in just about every respect. For example, a block plane has a single cutter rather than a cutter paired with a cap iron, and the cutter is positioned bevel up. All this adds up to a precision tool designed specifically to plane end grain. Start by disassembling your block plane. Undo the cap and remove the cutter iron or blade. Inspect the bevel for nicks. Polish the back of the cutter, and hone the beveled edge. Have a look at the blade advance mechanism—brush out the dust and dribble a few drops of light oil on the screw thread. Make sure that the mouth is clean so that the cutter sits level. Go over the plane, cleaning all the faces. Finally, put the plane back together, and adjust the cutter for a fine skimming cut.

See also: stripping down / solution 1 / page 108

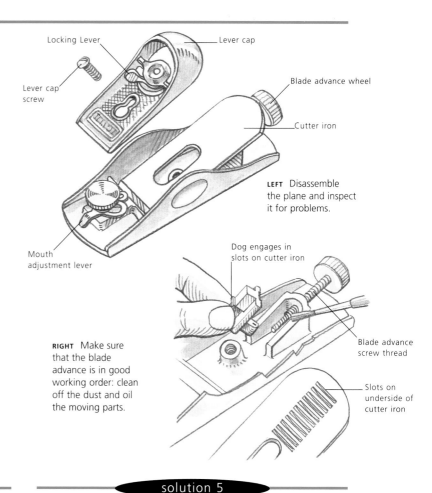

Locking Lever — Lever cap
Lever cap screw
Blade advance wheel
Cutter iron
Mouth adjustment lever

LEFT Disassemble the plane and inspect it for problems.

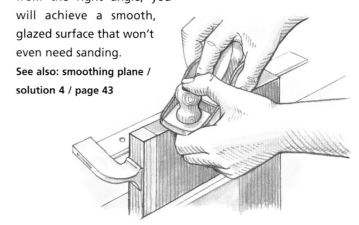

Dog engages in slots on cutter iron
Blade advance screw thread
Slots on underside of cutter iron

RIGHT Make sure that the blade advance is in good working order: clean off the dust and oil the moving parts.

solution 4

CUTTING A MITER

One of the easiest ways of preventing grain splitting off is to chisel off the far end of the wood at a mitered angle. Mark the end with a square and knife—so that the desired level is clear to see—and then pare the corner off with a chisel. The wood can either be worked in the vise as shown, or trimmed on a shooting board. Either way, you must be careful not to cut below the scribed line.

See also: miter / solution 1 / page 34

LEFT Clamp the wood firmly–not too high up in the vise–and plane down to the desired level using a block plane. The bevel at the end of the stroke will reduce the chance of splitting.

solution 5

PLANING AT A SKEWED ANGLE

Planing at a skewed or shearing angle is another technique used for smoothing end grain. The plane is held firmly so that you can put all the power of your shoulder behind the stroke, and you angle the plane to make a slightly sideways shearing cut. If the cutter is properly honed and you approach the grain from the right angle, you will achieve a smooth, glazed surface that won't even need sanding.

See also: smoothing plane / solution 4 / page 43

ABOVE Try various paring angles to find one that works best on your piece of wood.

16 I put several boards through the planer, and they are all slightly rippled. How can I redo them?

ABOVE Angle the workpiece to the light to highlight the degree of ripple.

solution 1

LEFT If the knives are not parallel, there will be a difference between the carry-forward distance of the two sticks.

ADJUSTING THE CUTTERHEAD

A good starting point is to check that the knives are parallel to the outfeed table. First switch off the power and pull out the plug, and warn everyone what you are doing. Then lay two sticks across the cutterhead, and make a mark on both sticks at the beginning or lip of the outfeed table. Carefully turn the cutterhead so that the first knife lifts and carries the two sticks forward and sets them down. Again make a mark at the lip of the outfeed table. Use a gauge or metal rule to measure the roll-forward distance on both sticks. If they are identical, the knife is parallel to the outfeed table. If not, then the knife needs resetting. Resetting is easily done by undoing the holding nuts and easing the knife little by little until it is parallel. Repeat the procedure for the remaining knives. WARNING—For safety's sake, you must make absolutely sure that all the cutterhead holding nuts are tight before plugging in and turning on the planer.

See also: caring for blades / solution 3 / page 38

solution 2

SAFELY FEEDING THE WORKPIECE

The planer is potentially a very dangerous power tool. The safest control procedure, especially on pieces shorter than 10 in., is to use a notched push stick—a stick with a V-shaped notch at the business end. In use, the guard is set as low as possible, and the workpiece is put down on the table and pushed through—with the stick pushing down at the infeed end, and the fingers pressing down on the wood as it emerges. The trick is to balance the pressure so that the wood is guided through the planer rather than forced.

See also feather board jig / solution 8 / page 124

solution 3

CHECKING THE BELTS

If the wood you power-plane is rippled, it might be that the belts are slipping. To check for this, first switch off the power and pull out the plug. Remove the casing and arrange a light so that you can see what you are doing. Brush away the dust. Check the tension of the belt by trying to pull it around the wheel. If it slips it is too slack, so make sure that the springs are in place. Most machines have simple adjustments that allow you to increase or maintain belt tension. If the belt is glazed or cracked, or the layers are peeling, it is time to buy a new belt.

See also: tuning / solution 4 / page 39

LEFT Exert a balanced downward pressure and forward thrust.

solution 4

USING A SMOOTHING PLANE

All machine-planed wood needs to be worked further with a hand plane. I say this because no matter the quality of your planer, the wood will be to some slight degree rippled. If you want to achieve perfect boards—and have fun along the way—then you need to master the age-old technique of smoothing with a hand plane. Take your smoothing plane—either a wood or a metal one—and spend some time making sure that the cutting edge is parallel to the mouth and set for the finest skimming cut. Make sure that the corners of the blade have been rounded over. Set the board to be planed flat on the bench, butt it against a stop, and start at the end of the board nearest you, skimming off the high spots. Work with a slanted stroke along the length of the board. It's a straightforward planing procedure, so long as the blade is set for the very finest shallow cut.

See also: skewed plane / solution 5 / page 41

LEFT Advance the blade only enough to make the lightest of skimming cuts. With this particular plane it is also possible to adjust the width of the mouth.

LEFT Work at a shearing angle, all the while backing up towards the end nearest you.

solution 5

USING A CABINET SCRAPER

If you want to achieve the best surface, you must use a scraper. The important thing about the scraper is not so much how it is used—because that is soon learned by trial and error—but rather how it is sharpened. To sharpen the scraper, secure it in a vise and square off the edge with a fine-grooved file. Next hold it vertically on an oilstone, and rub the edge until it is perfectly smooth and square. This done, lay the scraper face down on the stone and burnish one side; then flip it over and burnish the other. Finally, set the scraper back in the vise, and take a tool like a gouge or screwdriver, and run it at an angle along the edge so as to raise the burr. In use, the scraper is flexed with your thumbs—so that it bends away from you—and you lean it forward and push it away from you. As you cut, you adjust the angle and the direction of the stroke for the best bite.

See also: diamond stone / solution 3 / page 106

        scraper / solution 2 / page 59

        scraping / solution 2 / page 16

LEFT Note that it is the burr produced on both sides that is used for cutting.

RIGHT Make adjustments to the holding angle and the direction of the stroke for the best cut.

17 I want to build a table from quarter-sawn white oak, but it is very expensive! Also, I am worried that the 4 x 4 in. solid legs might split and/or warp. How can I do the project less expensively? And how can I ensure that the legs stay true?

RIGHT The finished, hollow mitered leg.

HOLLOW QUARTER-SAWN MITERED LEGS

You might be able to save costs by building the legs up from thinner sections of quarter-sawn wood. Building mitered legs is a good way to do this.

1 You want four 30-in. long 4 x 4-in. square-section legs. Allowing for wood lost to sawing and planing, you need for each leg four pieces ¾ in. thick, 4¼ in. wide and 32 in. long—a total length of 512 in. Plane one side and both edges to a smooth, flat surface. Aim for a finished size of ⅝ in. thick and 4 in. wide.

2 Set your table saw to make a 45° miter cut—using either a tilting table or a tilting arbor—and pass each width through so that the two edges are cut at 45° in from the finished face. If you tilt the blade towards the fence, be careful that it doesn't bind or pinch.

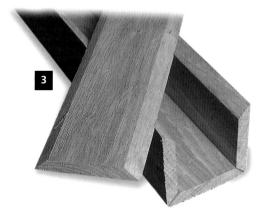

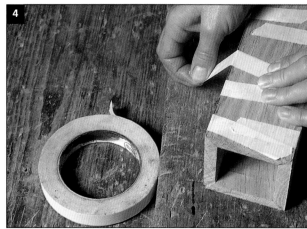

3 When you have cut all four sides, do a trial assembly to see how they go together. Arrange them for best fit. Then spread glue on mating faces and start assembling. The easiest way is to build up three of the sides like an open-ended box, and then add the fourth side.

4 Clamp the workpiece with fabric strap clamps or strips of masking tape. Test for squareness. Note— depending on the design of your table, you might well need to plug the ends of the legs. Best to use oak plugs and put them in at the glue stage.

See also: table saw / solutions 1–6 / pages 118–19

LAMINATED LEGS

Though on the face of it, laminating the legs up from thin sections might seem to be expensive, you can cut costs by using several thicknesses and widths, and by using flawed wood in the central core. As long as the faces of the legs look good and the legs are structurally sound, there is no reason why the cores can't be made up from throwaway wood. In addition, laminating the legs will free you from worries about their warping.

ABOVE This laminated leg conceals that fact that the central layers are made from inexpensive second-choice wood.

1 Staying with the same scenario of building 30 in. long 4 x 4 in. square legs from quarter-sawn oak, saw all your wood to length. Plane every length so that it is true on all faces and edges.

2 Spend time playing around with the wood and arranging it in 4¼ in. high stacks 4¼ in. wide. Each stack should have a good board at top and bottom, with the core arranged so that its best edges are presented at the side of the stack. If you are using a mix of narrow widths for the core, then do your best to ensure that they are staggered so that the seams do not match.

3 When you have assembled the four stacks that go to make a leg, do a trial run, and see where the clamps should be positioned. If you are short of clamps, consider using a quick-setting glue. Tighten up the clamps and see how the laminations go together. Plan the procedure so that nothing is left to chance. When you are happy with the clamping arrangement, then take it apart, spread glue on mating faces and clamp it all together again.

4 When the glue is fully dry, plane the legs down to 4 x 4-in. square sections.

See also: laminating / solution 2 / page 27

ABOVE The finished leg. The veneers can be mitered at the corners or lapped and planed back.

HOLLOW LEGS COVERED WITH HAND-SAWN VENEERS

If you want to cut the cost to a minimum, building hollow legs and covering them with hand-sawn oak veneer is the best way to proceed.

1 Take your quarter-sawn oak and resaw and plane it to a thickness of about ⅛ in. You need four sheets about 4¼ in. wide for each leg. As for the core, it can be made up from just about any wood that is at hand, so long as it's well seasoned and sound. I decided to make my hollow core from 1¼ in. thick pine. Plane the core so that all mating faces are true.

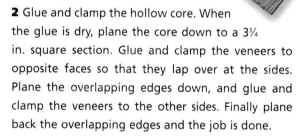

2 Glue and clamp the hollow core. When the glue is dry, plane the core down to a 3¾ in. square section. Glue and clamp the veneers to opposite faces so that they lap over at the sides. Plane the overlapping edges down, and glue and clamp the veneers to the other sides. Finally plane back the overlapping edges and the job is done.

See also: veneer / solution 4 / page 73

ABOVE While this method does require a lot of planning and planing, using veneer reduces the cost of expensive wood to a minimum.

LEFT While the veneers can be mitered at the corners, the easiest way is to butt-join them so there is a generous overlap, and then plane them back.

Chisels

Beginners tend to take the chisel for granted. What they fail to understand is that there are many different kinds of chisels, each designed for a specific range of operations. If you are making unsatisfactory joints, the chances are you are making inappropriate cuts with a poorly chosen chisel. The following solutions will put more power into your chiseling elbow.

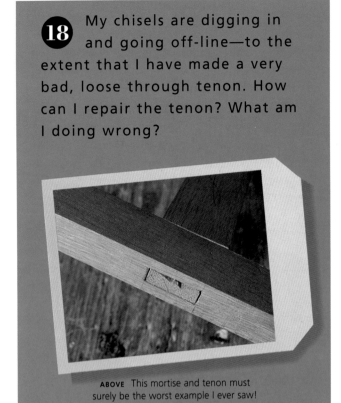

18 My chisels are digging in and going off-line—to the extent that I have made a very bad, loose through tenon. How can I repair the tenon? What am I doing wrong?

ABOVE This mortise and tenon must surely be the worst example I ever saw!

---
solution 1

AVOID MAKING LARGE CUTS
A common mistake made by enthusiastic beginners is taking chisel cuts that are far too deep and then levering up with the handle. The end result is a splintered mess with too much wood chiseled away. The best procedure is to shave only a thin layer with each stroke, working carefully down to the mark.

---
solution 2

PACKING A TENON
If you have cut a loose tenon, a quick repair is to pack the joint with thin shims.

1 Look at the size of the gaps in the joint—maybe you need only fill two sides.

2 Use a chisel to cut slivers of matching wood. Each should be wide enough to fill the gap and be slightly tapered or wedge-shaped.

3 Squirt glue into the gap, and slide the wedges in until they are tight.

4 Let the glue dry, and then plane the workpiece smooth.

See also: tenon / solution 2 / page 3

ANATOMY OF A CHISEL

You need top-quality chisels! The generic chisel is a flat-bladed tool made up of a long, straight blade that has a cutting edge on one end and a handle on the other. While there are many families of chisels, there are only three basic types—the tanged chisel that has a tang running from the bolster into a wooden handle, the modern chisel with a stub shaft running into a molded plastic handle, and the socket chisel with a wooden handle fitting into a socket. The length and structure of the blade and the way the blade fits into the handle equates with the quality and the life expectancy of the tool.

See also: storage / solution 3 / page 11

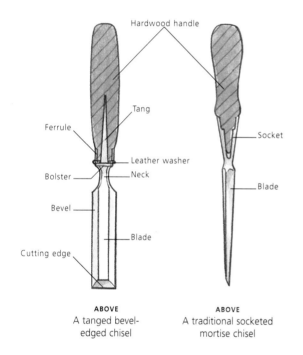

Hardwood handle

Tang

Ferrule

Socket

Leather washer

Bolster — **Neck**

Bevel — **Blade**

Blade

Cutting edge

ABOVE	ABOVE
A tanged bevel-edged chisel	A traditional socketed mortise chisel

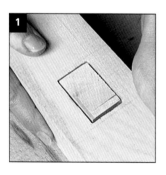

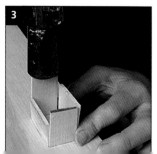

COMMON CHISEL TYPES

While there are dozens of chisel types—each designed for a specific task —there are only three types of chisels in common use: the firmer chisel, the bevel-edged chisel, and the mortise chisel.

SHEFFIELD: 3/4" 20 mm :ENGLAND

Firmer chisel

■ **FIRMER CHISELS:** The firmer chisel with its rectangular, straight-sided blade is strong enough to be driven with a mallet. It is designed for general-purpose, everyday work.

SHEFFIELD: 3/4" 20 mm :ENGLAND

Bevel-edged chisel

■ **BEVEL-EDGED CHISELS:** The bevel-edged chisel, sometimes called a paring chisel, has a blade beveled on both sides. It is designed for paring and joinery. The beveled edges allow you to chisel into tight corners without the blade binding.

SHEFFIELD :13 mm 1/2: ENGLAND

Mortise chisel

■ **MORTISE CHISELS:** The mortise chisel is characterized by having a heavy, straight-sided blade tapered from front to back along its length. There are two kinds, a heavy-duty one for cutting deep mortises and for house framing, and a lighter version used for general joinery.

USING A CHISEL

There are three primary chisel cuts: vertical paring, horizontal paring and mallet-driven cutting.

■ **VERTICAL PARING:** Clamp the workpiece flat down on the workbench. Grip the bevel-edged chisel with your right hand, so that it is at right angles to your forearm. Place your left hand, knuckles down, on the workpiece so that your forefinger is behind the mark. Back the cutting edge of the chisel up to the mark, and then control the cut by hooking your right thumb around the chisel blade. Push the chisel down with your right shoulder.

ABOVE Use the thumb and fingers of one hand to set the chisel on the mark, and the grip of the other hand to power the thrust.

■ **HORIZONTAL PARING:** Secure the workpiece in a vise—or hold it down with a clamp. Take the chisel in your right hand so that the handle butts into your palm, and your forefinger points down the length of the blade. Put the knuckles of your left hand down so that the length of your forefinger is resting against the side of the workpiece, and lay the back of the chisel blade on the pads of your fingers. Nip the blade with your left-hand thumb and forefinger, place the cutting edge to the mark, and push to cut.

Put your shoulder into the stroke.

■ **MALLET CUTS:** Clamp the workpiece flat down on the workbench. Take the chisel in your left hand with your fingers wrapped around the handle in a comfortable grip. Use your right hand to position the blade edge on the mark. Take the mallet in your right hand and strike the top of the handle a well-aimed blow. The important part of this procedure is taking care to position the blade precisely on the mark.

See also: **controlled paring / solution 2 / page 49**

ABOVE Place the blade on the mark and use the mallet to strike a careful blow.

ABOVE Use one hand to set the blade on the mark, and the other hand and shoulder to power the thrust.

---

19 I have botched one half of a half-lap—it is too deep. How can I cut the other half to fit?

ABOVE The faulty half of the joint, with the scrap on the wrong side of the drawn line.

CUTTING THE OTHER HALF TO COMPENSATE

The best way to rescue the job is to cut the second half-lap more shallowly to make up the difference.

Mark the cut line of the second lap directly from the lap that you have already done, and then pare carefully (see right for descriptions of good paring technique) and refit until the joint comes together successfully.

See also: **controlled paring / solution 2 / page 49**

ABOVE RIGHT Cut the other half of the joint shallow to compensate for the overly deep half.

solution 2

CONTROLLED PARING

Good cross and half-laps are achieved primarily by careful, controlled horizontal paring. Good paring skills can only be achieved with practice and more practice. If you want to bone up your paring skills, take a length of 2 x 2 in. hardwood, run a couple of saw cuts down to a gauged line—say 1 in. deep and 2 in. apart—and secure it in a vise. Now, take a well-honed 1 in. wide bevel-edged chisel, set the cutting edge a shade lower than the surface of the wood, hold the chisel blade level, and make a careful forward stroke. If you have done it right, the shaving will be paper-thin. And so you continue, repeating the stroke, until you are able to do it with ease.

See also: using a chisel / solution 5/ page 48

ABOVE Practice paring out scrap until you are able to do it quickly and surely.

solution 3

CUTTING IN FROM THE SIDES

The correct procedure for cutting a lap joint in from the sides is to mark the joint out with a knife and square, and then carefully make two saw cuts that run down on the scrap side and stop just short of the gauge line. Then cut away the scrap using horizontal paring cuts made with a chisel angled to the left and right of center. Work little by little, first from one side of the wood and then from the other, until you finish up with a little roof-shaped piece of scrap at the middle. The skill is being able to make the cuts one after the other so that the scrap comes away as fine shavings, and the surface of the scrap is angled from the center down to meet at the intersection of the saw cut and the gauged line.

See also: mortise gauge / solution 2 / page 31

RIGHT Tilt the blade slightly to leave a ridge-shaped piece of scrap at the center.

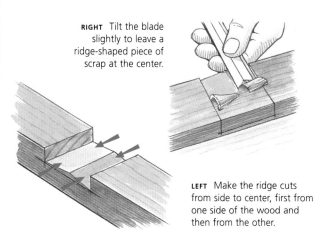

LEFT Make the ridge cuts from side to center, first from one side of the wood and then from the other.

solution 4

LEFT Chisel with a forward side-to-side shearing action.

SKIMMING

While skimming is a general term that is used to describe fine horizontal paring, it is also more specifically a term that describes the final stage of cutting a lap. The skill of skimming has to do with being able to advance the chisel with a forward pivoting or skewing action that slices through the wood with a shearing cut. In action, set the chisel at a horizontal angle, drop the handle slightly so that the cutting edge tilts up, and then push it forward with a scything stroke. As the peak of scrap gets lower, lift the handle up. Finally, complete the lap by setting the cutting edge in the center of the gauged line and skimming first from one side of the wood and then from the other.

See also: chisels / solution 5 / page 48

20 I have just cut a bad dovetail—it is too loose. How can I compensate to make it fit? How can I avoid the problem the next time?

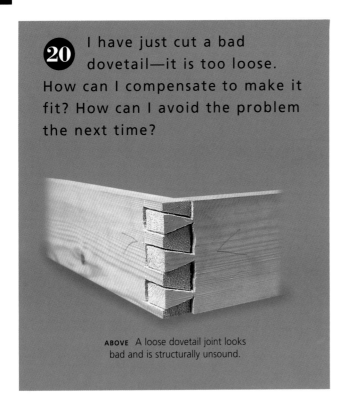

ABOVE A loose dovetail joint looks bad and is structurally unsound.

solution 1

VENEERING A LOOSE DOVETAIL

If you have cut a loose dovetail, a quick remedy is to apply strips of veneer to the faces and then trim.

1 Study the joint, and decide whether the pins or the tails are at fault. Select veneers to match the color of the bad faces.

2 You have a choice at this stage—do you want to glue the veneers to the badly cut faces before the joint is assembled? Or do you want to put the joint together and use the veneers in much the same way as wedged shims? I decided to go for the shims. Glue and assemble the joint, then apply glue and slide in the veneer shims. Use a gap-filling glue if the mistake is serious.

3 When the glue is dry, use a chisel to pare the veneer ends flush.

See also: dovetails / solution 2 / page 50

solution 2

BASIC OPEN DOVETAILS

To my way of thinking, the dovetail is the perfect joint for small boxes, trays, chests and drawers. Not only is it one of the strongest methods of joining two boards together at right angles, but better yet, it is attractive and decorative. And not only that, cut-

ABOVE A simple open dovetail is both strong and attractive. Note how the ends of the tails and the pins are cut slightly long so that they can be cut back as needed at finish.

ting dovetails is a skill-testing challenge that shouldn't be missed. And just in case you are thinking that there is some big secret about cutting dovetails— some piece of pithy wisdom that sums up the whole technique, or a mantra that you can repeat— there is! The magic words are patience, practice and precision. The only other thing to remember here is that there are just about as many ways of cutting a dovetail as there are woodworkers. The following is just one way to proceed:

1 First prepare the wood so that all the faces, edges and ends are true. Then take pencil, ruler, bevel gauge and knife and carefully lay out the shape and position of the dovetails. Shade in the scrap areas to avoid miscutting. Use a dovetail saw to make cuts down to the shoulder line, then remove the end scrap with the tenon saw. Cut out the bulk of the shaded scrap with a coping saw, and then pare the sawed faces to a smooth surface.

2 Clamp the second piece in a vise with a scrap piece laid on the bench, and position the first piece so that it is perfectly square and aligned. Use the point of a sharp knife to trace the shape of the joint.

3 Mark in the shoulder line, and extend vertical lines down the front of the joint. Then take the dovetail saw and cut on the scrap side of the line down to the shoulder line.

4 Now, just as before, use the coping saw to remove the scrap from between the pins. Be sure to cut well to the scrap side of the shoulder line.

5 Put a strong piece of scrap wood behind the second board, clamp them both in the vise, and use a sharp chisel to pare all the sawed faces.

6 When you have assembled the joint so that the two boards come together for a good fit, then glue and clamp it, and when dry clean up the outside of the joint with a plane. Work out from the corner so as to avoid splitting the end grain.

See also: dovetails / solution 2 / page 61

Marking
gauge line

1″ D   D   1″

Socket

¼″
¼″
¼″
¼″
¼″
¼″
¼″
¼″

FRONT   SIDE

Full pin   Half pin

1″

PLAN

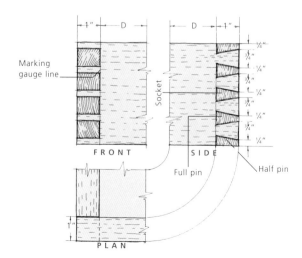

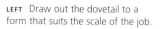

LEFT Draw out the dovetail to a
form that suits the scale of the job.

ABOVE An angled block of wood clamped to the workpiece can be used as a guide for the saw.

SLIDING DOVETAILS

The sliding dovetail is one step on from the housed sliding joint. The procedure is as follows: Two parallel lines are squared across the wood, the lines are cut with the saw held against the angled guide block at an angle of about 80°, and the scrap is removed with a paring chisel and hand router or side rabbet plane. The dovetail batten is worked with the saw, chisel and a side rabbet plane to fit the housing. The procedure is to mark out the dovetail with a pencil ruler and square, cut the shoulder line in with a fine-bladed saw, then clean up the dovetail with the side rabbet plane. If you don't have either the hand router or the side rabbet plane, then you can use a fine paring chisel.

See also: sliding dovetail/ solution 4 / page 69

LEFT While this example of a sliding dovetail is adequate, the knot is not so clever!

BLIND MITER DOVETAIL

Of all the dovetails, the full blind miter is considered by many to be the most challenging. Though in essence it's much the same as the through dovetail, the difference is that the shape and structure of the joint is hidden within the miter. The obvious question is, why go to such trouble when the beauty of the joint is going to be hidden? The answer is, the pleasure is in the doing. The procedure is as follows:

Scribe the thickness of the wood on the end of both boards. Run a line across the diagonal to mark out the mating faces of the 45° miter. About one third in from what will be the outside corner, sink a rabbet about one third down towards the shoulder line—but stop just short of the mitered line. Use a chisel to clear the miter end, then lay out the pins. Make saw cuts across the miter to mark out the socket, and then pare out the scrap. Finally, use the pins to mark the position of the tails on the other board, and cut the dovetails in much the same way as described above.

See also: correct chisels / solution 4 / page 47

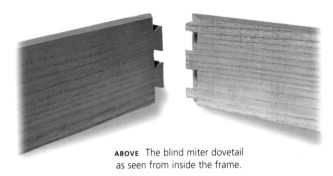

ABOVE The blind miter dovetail as seen from inside the frame.

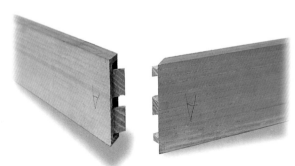

ABOVE In a blind dovetail the pins and tails are completely hidden in the mitered joint.

21 I am making a frame, and have broken the tenon off in the mortise. How can I remove the broken stub? How can I repair the joint?

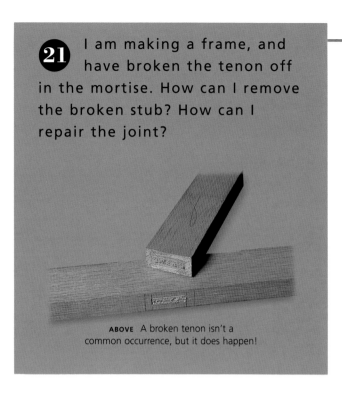

ABOVE A broken tenon isn't a common occurrence, but it does happen!

ABOVE RIGHT Make sure that the stub is a push fit, and then glue and clamp it in the slot.

solution 1

FITTING A STUB TENON

First, drill three or four holes through the broken tenon to clear out most of it. Use one of your less precious chisels to chip out the rest of the waste stub and the hard glue, and then use a good mortise chisel to clean up the sides of the mortise. If need be, make the mortise slightly larger. This done, cut the damage done to the other broken piece back to the shoulder. Run two parallel saw cuts in to a depth of about 2 in. and wide enough to match the new mortise. Very carefully pare the waste out from between the two saw cuts, so that you finish up with a clean slot. Cut a new tenon stub to fit the mortise, and then glue and clamp it into the slot. After the glue is dry, plane the sides smooth before regluing the tenon into the mortise.

See also: wedging a tenon / solution 2 / page 46

solution 2

CONVERT TO A BOLT AND TOGGLE FITTING

If you are making a piece of functional furniture for your workshop, say, it might be better to skip the joinery and use a metal bolt and toggle. Let the glue dry, and use the chisel and plane to clean the damaged stub back to the surface of the wood. Clamp the two members together—as if they were jointed—and establish the end-center point of the through tenon by drawing crossed diagonals. Select a drill bit size to fit the diameter of your threaded rod, and run a hole through the tenon stub and into the tenon member to a depth of about 2½ in. Select a drill bit to fit the diameter of the toggle, and then about 2 in. along the tenon member, run another hole to intersect your first hole at right angles. Finally, set the toggle in place so that the threaded hole is aligned, pass the threaded rod through the joint, attach the brass cap, and tighten it up with an Allen key.

See also: bolt-fitting / solution 3 / page 121

patent fixing / solution 4 / page 61

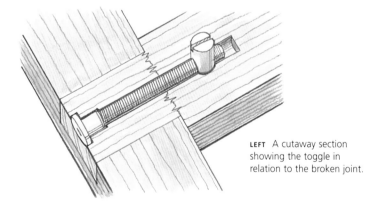

LEFT A cutaway section showing the toggle in relation to the broken joint.

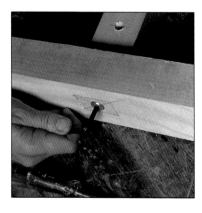

LEFT Tightened up with the Allen key, the finished toggle joint is an attractive solution.

Routers

While there is no denying that the power router has changed the face of twentieth-century woodwork, there are thousands of power router owners out there who never get anywhere near realizing the full potential of what has been described as the most versatile woodworking power tool ever. If your router is not doing just what you expect it to do, then perhaps we have some answers.

22 I am having a hard time with my router doing decorative edge cuts freehand. Is there a better way?

ABOVE This particular router edge mess obviously needs to be redone!

USE TEMPLATES AND TEMPLATE GUIDES

You can upgrade the performance of your router by fitting a template guide bushing. Template guide bushings are metal or plastic tubes or sleeves fitted to the router base by screws or locking nuts. The template guide bushing sticks out in such a way that the router bit passes through without touching it. In action, the template guide bushing is pressed against the template and the router is run around the template in such a way that the bit is always the same distance from the edge of the template. Or put another way, when the template guide bushing is pressed against the template, it will guide the router so that the bit is always the same distance from and parallel to the template.

Though in many ways the template guide bushing performs the same function as a tipped bit or a bit with a follower bearing, the template guide bushing is sturdier and more reliable—it won't fail. While the template-guide system is relatively inexpensive and easy to attach, it is to my mind not ideal because you have to think ahead and make allowance for the increased distance between the cutting edge of the bit and the guiding edge of the template. It's no big deal, but it does mean that when you make the template, you must make it slightly bigger than the desired workpiece. And of course you must also bear in mind that the template guide bushing is always the slave of the template. If the edge of the template has dips and bumps, then the template guide bushing will cause the router bit to reproduce them faithfully.

See also: turret stops / solution 5 / page 57

Subbases are screwed to the base of the router. Do not over-tighten these otherwise you will strip the threads

RIGHT Having chosen what you consider to be a suitable subbase, spend time making sure that it is well put together.

LEFT Measure the template guide to make sure that it relates to the thickness of the subbase, the desired depth of cut, and the type and size of bit you intend to use.

BELOW Make sure that the guide is held up against the template.

BUILD YOUR OWN SUBBASE

A subbase is a thin sheet of super-smooth plastic or compound fitted onto the base of the router, and on which the router travels. Subbases come in all manner of shapes and designs—round, rectangular, with circular holes cut out, and so on. One problem with some routers is the fact that the subbase, as supplied, may block your view of your work—either it is made of an opaque material, or the bit hole is so small that you can't see what's going on. This is especially not a good idea when you are trying to work freehand. If this is the case, then you need to build or buy an auxiliary subbase to replace the one supplied with the machine.

The advantage of replacing the router subbase with one of your own is that while manufacturers tend to give you the minimum, you will be able to design a subbase customized to fit your specific needs. So you can make one of see-through acrylic, or you can make one with large openings, or whatever—either way you will find it easier if you can see where you are going. If your router's subbase is attached with screws, then you have no problem—you just copy the pattern of its screw holes, unscrew it, and replace it with your custom one. But if it is cemented on, then it is better to leave it in place and attach your customized subbase to it with double-sided sticky tape—the type used to hold down carpets.

See also: router use / solution 1 / page 58

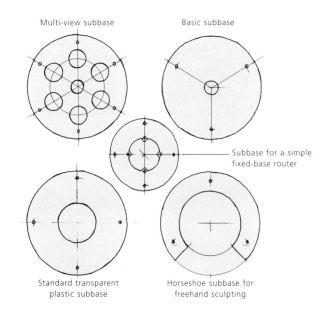

Multi-view subbase

Basic subbase

Subbase for a simple fixed-base router

Standard transparent plastic subbase

Horseshoe subbase for freehand sculpting

ABOVE There will come a time when you need to make subbases to suit your own needs, which is when the fun starts.

23 In cutting with my router, I find myself burning the edges. How can I remove the burn marks? What went wrong?

ABOVE One thing you can say about a router friction burn is that it can't be repaired with a piece of sandpaper.

solution 1

OVERCUTTING

The first thing that you have to understand is that a router burn is almost invariably glazed, and as a result it is almost impossible to sand away. While there are several possible causes for the burn—dealt with in the next couple of sections—the best way of removing it is to cut it away with another pass. You can redesign the project slightly, and then saw the edge off and re-run the router around it. If this is impossible, you might make a slightly deeper cut that runs over and removes the burn. If this is also impossible, then you might fit a slightly larger bit and take a second run over the first.

See also: feed / solution 4 / page 57

finishing edges / solution 1 / page 70

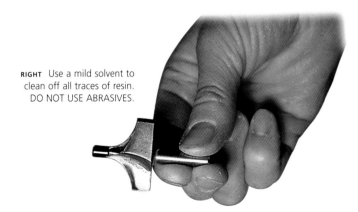

RIGHT Use a mild solvent to clean off all traces of resin. DO NOT USE ABRASIVES.

solution 2

SHARPENING

If on close inspection you see that the bit edge is dull—perhaps because you have used it to work a man-made material that contains bit-blunting resin glue—then it is possible to sharpen the cutting edges slightly by careful honing.

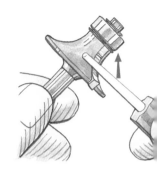

The key word here is slightly. First establish whether your bit is made from high-speed steel or carbide steel. If it is carbide, then take a small diamond hone and work around the bit, just stroking each cutting face in turn. If it is high-speed steel, then use a diamond hone as before, only this time go at it much more cautiously. Stay away from pilots and bearings, and make sure to hone each of the cutters an even amount. If in using the router you find that, however careful you were, the bit is off-balance and causing a vibration, then for safety's sake send it out to be professionally honed.

ABOVE RIGHT Hone the cutting edges to a bright finish. Treat both cutters equally.

solution 3

CHECKING FOR A BUILDUP OF RESIN AND DEBRIS

Have a good look at your bits and check them out for a buildup of resin. Resin is the sticky substance that oozes out of some woods. When it builds up on the bits, it forms a black glaze-like coating that causes the bit to overheat. Once this starts to happen, a whole sequence of events occurs—the bit is difficult to fit, it tends to run off-balance, the glaze burns the wood being worked, and so on. This all sounds bad, but the whole problem can be quickly corrected by using oven cleaner to remove the resin. Protect the clean bit with a smear of light engine oil. WARNING—Never use an abrasive to scrape the shank, or to clean out the collets.

solution 4

CHECKING THE DIRECTION AND RATE OF FEED

In a good many instances, burns are caused by changes in the rate of feed. If you slow down or come to a stop, or your progress is hesitant, then the bit whirs away on the spot and heats up the resins in the wood, and burns the wood. It's not easy to say what particular rate of feed is best, because so many different factors enter into deciding the optimum rate—for example, the state of the wood you are working (hard, soft, sticky, damp or whatever), the run of the grain in relationship to the direction of the cut, the size and power of your router, the shape and design of your bit, the depth and width of the cut, whether you are running a straight edge, an outside corner, an inside corner, or a complex curve,

and so on. Given all that, the general rule of thumb is the faster the better. Of course your setup has to be safe, but overall, a fast feed causes fewer problems than a slow one does. If you have any doubts about this, then it's a good idea to have a trial run with a scrap piece of the same wood and the same bit you intend using for the project. Working in this way, you will build up your confidence and generally be able to judge when everything is going all right. As to direction, you should always feed against the bit rotation—meaning that when you are moving forward, the edge being worked is to the left of the cutter.

see also: friction burn / solution 1 / page 56

templates / solution 1 / page 54

solution 5

TURRET STOPS

If you are having feed and burn problems, it may well be that you are trying to take too deep a cut. The best advice here is to make the cut with two or three passes instead of one. This is easily done by setting the mechanism known as a rotating stop block, or a rotating turret. All this is, in effect, is a small cluster of screws—usually three—that are mounted on the top side of the router base. If you look closely, you will see that the screws are set at three different heights, with each screw having its own micro adjustment. In use, the stop rod is lowered and set to the depth of the cut. The distance between the bottom of the rod and the top of the screw equals the depth of the cut. When you come to make the three-stage cut, you make the first pass until

the rod comes to rest on the first screw, then you turn the turret around for the next deeper setting, and so on. The turret stop allows you to map out the sequence of depths in advance.

see also: router groove / solution 1 / page page 58

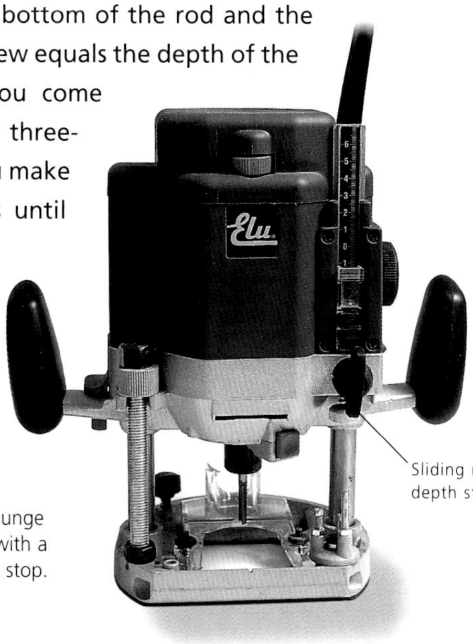

A sliding rod (shown in the picture on the left) is held at this point on the body of the router. The depth scale on the side of the router acts as an aid to setting the turret stops.

The "stops" are three height-adjustable screws of different length. When plunging, the end of the sliding rod hits the head of one of these screws which stops the router from cutting deeper.

The screws are mounted in this revolving turret. Select one of three pre-set cutting depths by turning the turret to a new position

Sliding rod depth stop

RIGHT A typical plunge router, complete with a three-screw turret stop.

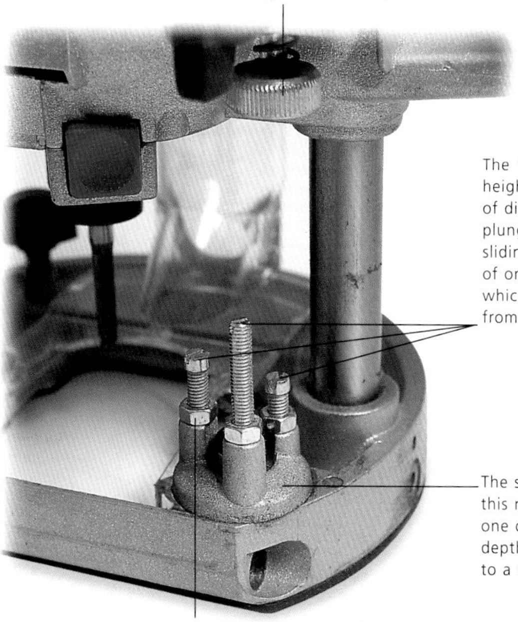

Locking nuts ensure the screws do not move after they are set

ABOVE Check the turret stop to make sure that all the screws and locknuts are in place and working.

24. I have butt-jointed two boards. The seam does not look good. What can I do to improve it?

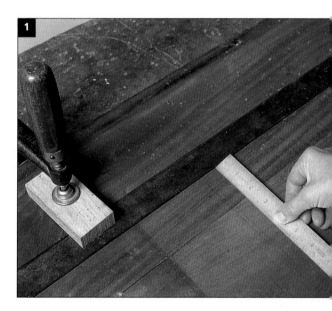

ABOVE A butt joint with gaps looks bad.

ROUTING A COVER-UP GROOVE

One of the best ways to conceal a bad butt joint is to route a decorative bead over the joint. Of course it doesn't do too much for structural integrity, but at least you have boards looking as if they had been done that way on pupose. The bead can be as simple or as fancy as you like—from a straightforward v-section groove, through to a full v-and-bead section. The procedure is as follows:

1 Choose a suitable bit, then clamp the workpiece securely to the bench. Clamp a straightedge to the workpiece so that it is parallel to the seam, and the distance between the straightedge and the seam matches the base of your router. Spend time with a square and measure making sure that the setup is right. When you are done, set your router on the guide and touch down—just to make absolutely sure that the center of the bit is right on target.

2 Finally, when you have checked and double checked that the guide is precisely where it needs to be, set the depth stop to fit the bit, switch on the power, and begin. You won't go far wrong as you are cutting if you make sure that the flat edge of the router base is always firmly up against the guide edge.

See also: router setting / solution 5 / page 57

solution 1

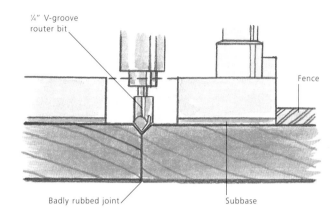

¼" V-groove router bit

Fence

Badly rubbed joint

Subbase

ABOVE A cross-sectional view showing a typical router setup.

solution 2

ROUTING A CHANNEL FOR A DECORATIVE INLAY

If the bad seam occurs in a surface that needs to be smooth—say for the top of a cabinet or table—then one good fix is to route a shallow slot over it and fit a decorative inlay into the slot.

1 First find a suitable inlay band. Then select a router bit of the appropriate width, and cut a trial slot in a piece of waste wood to establish the depth of the cut. The channel should be fractionally shallower than the thickness of the band, so that it stands slightly above the surface. It also should be a reasonably tight fit in the slot. Once you've worked this out, fit a straightedge guide to the joined boards and cut the channel.

2 Remove the router and the guide setup, and clear away all the dust and debris. Try the fit of the inlay band. If everything fits together well, the strip will stand slightly above the surface. When you are happy with the fit of the band, pull it out, spread glue on it and push it back into place.

3 Use the back of a hammer to press the inlay band firmly down into the channel.

4 Wipe up any excess glue with a slightly dampened cloth.

5 Finally, take a well-sharpened scraper and first cut the inlay band down to the level of the surface, and then scrape the whole surface to remove all traces of glue. Aim for a surface that is burnished to a sheen.

See also: scraper / solution 5 / page 43

solution 3

ROUTING A DOVETAIL GROOVE

If you are contemplating your goof and trying to think of a way out, but are not keen on decorative grooves or inlay bands, perhaps you could make a sliding dovetail strip. All you do is route a classic dovetail channel with the guide strip, as already described, then cut a strip to fit in the channel, glue

it in and plane it smooth. If you choose your wood and match the grain with care, you will achieve a nearly invisible seam. Or perhaps you can modify your design so that the routed dovetail is a feature. For example, if the boards are to be the front of a cabinet door or drawer, perhaps you can cut a groove and install a pull strip.

See also: sliding dovetail / solution 3 / page 52

Joints

A well-cut and close-fitting joint—
one that hisses out air when you
push it together—is one of the great
pleasures of woodworking. For many
woodworkers, the ability to make a
fine joint *is* woodworking. But if you
are one of those woodworkers who
fear the very prospect of cutting
joints, or if you have questions that
need to be answered, this is the
section for you.

25 I have just made a drawer
using dowel joints. It and I
are coming apart at the seams!
Where am I going wrong? How
can I repair the damage?

ABOVE Using dowels to joint a drawer front is a bad idea,
especially when the pulling forces are directly in line with the dowels.

solution 1

DESIGNING DOWEL JOINTS CORRECTLY

Dowel joints are a bad idea for making drawers—
especially when the dowels run parallel to the sides
into the front. By the very nature of things, not only
are the dowels going to be relatively short where
they fit into the drawer front, but worst still, every
time you pull on the drawer, you are pulling the
joint apart because you are pulling in line with the
dowels. If you have to keep the drawer as it is, then
put a false front on the inside, and run additional
dowels from and at right angles to the sides and into
the ends of the false front inside the drawer.

See also: drilling jig / solution 6 / page 123

RIGHT Fit a false
front inside the
drawer with glue
and screws, and
then run dowels
through from
the sides.

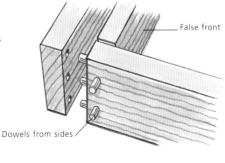

False front

Dowels from sides

solution 2

USE OF DOVETAILS

If you able to start over, then you can't do better than change the design and use dovetails. The wonderful thing about using dovetails for drawers is that the harder you pull at the drawer front, the more tightly the dovetails lock and hold. You could stay with dowels for the back joints, and have open dovetails on the front. If you don't want the joints to show, you can cover it up with a molding—as shown in the opening photograph—or you can use half-blind dovetails. If you enjoy a challenge, you can even use blind mitered dovetails.

See also: basic dovetails / solution 2 / page 50

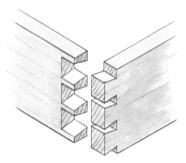

ABOVE If you are building a plain and simple drawer for a workshop, an open dovetail design is easy to make, structurally sound and it looks good.

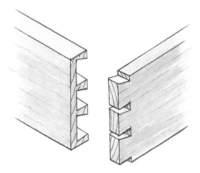

ABOVE A half-blind dovetail is a good joint for a structurally sound drawer with a plain front.

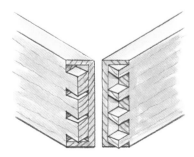

ABOVE Blind mitered dovetails are structurally sound but a challenge to cut. I think it is a pity the joint is hidden from view.

solution 3

REDESIGN

If you are committed to building the drawer with dowels, but are able to modify the design somewhat, you can give the drawer a thick front with an inside-drawer rabbet on the front panel. You can then run the dowels from the sides and into the rabbet—so that the dowels are aligned at right angles to the direction of the pull. You can spread the load and decrease the chance of splitting the drawer front by cutting down on the diameter of the dowels but having more of them.

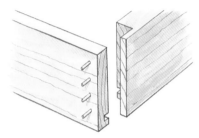

RIGHT While this design sticks with dowels, the rabbet and the use of smaller dowels in from the sides increases the glued surfaces and does not put the dowels in line with the pulling force.

solution 4

USING REINFORCEMENTS

If your drawers are finished and you cannot change the design, then I think that the best way to fix the problem is to strengthen the existing dowel joints with metal reinforcements—connecting bolts and metal cross-dowels, or threaded brass inserts with machine screws. Certainly some part of these reinforcements will show on the front of the drawer, but they are attractive in themselves, and they are amazingly strong. However, if you don't want them to show, you can recess them and hide the heads with wooden plugs glued into the recesses.

See also: toggle fitting / solution 2 / page 53

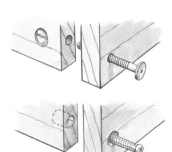

LEFT Metal dowel fittings are a good solution for making drawers that are structurally sound and attractive.

LEFT If you want the metal fittings hidden from view, you can use threaded brass inserts with machine screws, and cover the screws with wooden plugs.

26 I am making a large number of dowel joints. I have drilled the holes too deep —and some deeper than others! I need to ensure accuracy and consistency of dowel depth. And I need to make sure it doesn't happen again. How?

solution 1

USING A DRILL PRESS DEPTH STOP

One of the best and simplest ways of ensuring that a number of holes are all drilled to exactly the same depth is to use the in-built depth stop provided in the pinion shaft housing of a drill press. Loosen the locking tab handle, rotate the ring housing until the pointer lines up with the required depth—as written on the scale—and then tighten the lock handle. Finally, drill a hole in a piece of scrap and adjust the table height to suit. Once you have matched up the table height you lock it in place on the column and then drill away

See also: drill-press/ solution 6 / page 123

ABOVE Experiment with your drill press depth stop to find out how it works and its degree of accuracy.

solution 2

USING A TAPE MARK OR A STOP COLLAR

The importance of the exact depth of a drilled hole varies with the job. Sometimes you need only know approximately how deep a hole should be—it could be from 1 to 1¼ in. deep and it wouldn't matter too much—and other times you need to know that the hole is at a certain depth within a fraction of an inch either way.

If you want a quick and easy guide to mark hole depth, wrap a piece of masking tape around the drill bit at the required stop mark. If you need to bore a number of identical holes with a portable drill, use a little item known as a stop collar. You simply slide the collar on the bit and lock it in place with an Allen key.

See also: dowels / solution 1 / page 60

LEFT A patent stop collar attached to a twist bit. This one will countersink at the same time.

solution 3

MAKING A STOP BLOCK

If you want to be absolutely certain that a series of holes are all the same depth, then one of the easiest solutions is to make a stop block. Let's say that you want to drill a series of holes all ½ in. deep. You first drill a hole through a block of wood sized so that when you slide the block onto the drill bit ½ in. of the bit sticks out from the block. In use, the block will ensure that the hole runs no deeper than ½ in. If you have a complex project with a large number of holes at different depths and diameters, then simplify things as part of the setup by making a stop block for each of the various drill bits.

See also: dowels / solution 3 / page 61

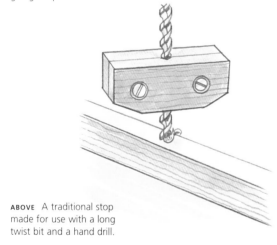

ABOVE A piece of tape wrapped around the drill bit does tell you when the depth is reached, it doesn't actually stop the drill from going deeper.

ABOVE A traditional stop made for use with a long twist bit and a hand drill.

LEFT The wood stop block actually prevents the bit going deeper. This method remains accurate as long as the drill bit does not slip in the chuck.

solution 4

MAKING A DEPTH JIG

If you want to insert dowels so that they protrude all the same height—meaning that the same length of each dowel sticks out from the hole—make a depth jig. This is a piece of wood the same thickness as the distance you want each dowel to stick out. Let's say that you want ½ in. of dowel to protrude. Drill a hole slightly larger than the dowel through a length of ½ in. wood. Push the dowel into its hole and set the jig over the dowel. Tap the dowel flush with the jig. The dowel will then protrude ½ in. from the surface of the workpiece.

See also: dowels / solution 1 / page 60

ABOVE Place the jig over the dowel and give the dowel a tap.

ABOVE It is plain to see that the amount of protruding dowel will always be equal to the thickness of the piece of wood.

27 I have installed a doorframe casing with mitered joints. The only problem is that the joints keep opening and closing with changing humidity. How can I stop this?

ABOVE Expansion and shrinkage across the width of the wood causes the joint to open and close.

solution 1

PAINT OR VARNISH TO STOP SHRINKAGE

Changes in humidity affect the moisture content of wood—and as the humidity goes up or down the wood expands or shrinks. This doesn't affect the length of a piece of wood very much but its width changes a good deal. Most joints are designed to open and close without showing expansion and shrinkage—tongue and groove joints, rabbets, dovetails and such—but glued and nailed butted miter joints are vulnerable. I would guess that your miter joints are located where they are subjected to noticeable changes in humidity. Perhaps there is damp air zipping through the doorway! While nothing can put a stop to changes in humidity—apart from the room being sealed and kept at a constant temperature—and if you are reluctant to change the kind of joint used in the casing, then the simplest solution is to give it a coat of paint, stain or varnish to protect it from the changes in moisture levels taking place in the room. I suggest that you wait for a dry day and for the gap in the joint to close up, and then apply a coat of sealer followed by a couple of coats of paint. This won't cure the problem altogether, but it will narrow the gap.

See also: **moisture / solution 2 / page 37**

solution 2

CUTTING THROUGH THE JOINT

The scenario here is that the joint has opened up, and while you are reluctant to remove the casing, you are prepared to cut into the joint.

1 Select a fillet of wood that is as thick as the widest part of the gap. Use a mortise saw and chisel to cut the joint open to the width of the fillet.

2 Aim for a good tight push-fit.

3 Use a coping saw to match the fillet to the profile of the casing.

4 When you are happy with the shape of the fillet, glue it in place, wait for the glue to dry, and then trim it back with a chisel. Seal the joint to lock out changes in humidity.

See also: **profile gauge / solution 2 / page 25**

solution 3

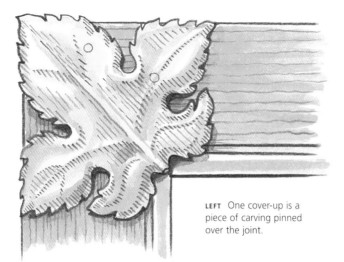

LEFT One cover-up is a piece of carving pinned over the joint.

INSTALLING A DECORATIVE TRIM

Another quick fix for the miter joint that keeps opening and closing is to borrow an idea from the past and cover the whole thing with a piece of suitable trim. This might be anything from a fragment of found carving to a piece of brassware. I once saw a cottage doorway where the owner had taken a piece of pierced brass from a broken dish and nailed it over the joints. Then again, I saw a doorway where some past woodworker had carved two little bows from lime wood, gilded them and nailed them, one on each side, over the miters. They looked great!

solution 4

ADDING CORNER BLOCKS

A traditional method of doing away with doorway miter joints is to fit corner blocks, usually with a rose or bullseye pattern. You see them all over—on the doorways of mansions, ordinary homes, Colonial houses, and so on. To my way of thinking, this is a beautifully simple solution. The molding just butts up to the block—no fancy joints, nothing to go wrong, and better yet, the blocks can be added to existing doorway casings with a minimum of cutting.

1 Mount a block on the lathe face plate and turn it to a suitable profile, or use a specially designed pattern bit in your router or drill press. Go for a simple shape—an inner peak and an outer ring.

2 In cross section the block should be slightly wider and slightly thicker than the molding—ideally about ½ in. wider. Choose a fine-grained hardwood like maple.

3 Set the finished block over the miter joint and mark the position with a pencil. Use a fine-bladed saw to cut out the ends of the miter. Be careful to avoid any hidden nails.

4 Set the blocks in place for a trial fit. Once you are happy that both blocks match, then glue and nail them in place. The blocks can be finished to match the casing, or better still, so that they contrast.

See also: finger rider jig / solution 10 / page 125

28 I made a plank tabletop and it has warped. How can I correct the warping? Is it possible to avoid warping in future projects?

ABOVE A metal straightedge shows the amount of twist and warp.

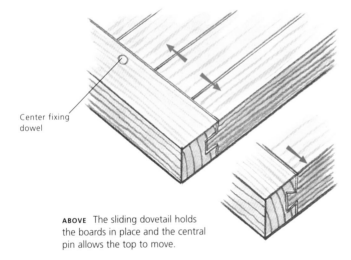

Center fixing dowel

ABOVE The sliding dovetail holds the boards in place and the central pin allows the top to move.

solution 1

SEASONING OF WOOD

In broad general terms, seasoning refers to the process of reducing the moisture content of wood slowly to allow it to shrink without warping, cracking and splitting. In the process of seasoning, wood dries out until its moisture content matches the humidity of its surroundings. Wood can be seasoned by natural airflow drying and by kiln drying.

Even after it is seasoned, wood will continue to gain or lose moisture to match the moisture content of its environment. If it is in a damp workshop it will swell up and grow, mostly in width, whereas if it is kept in your centrally heated home, then it will shrink. Because of this, you must try to gauge the difference between the humidity in your workshop and the humidity in your home. Ideally your workshop humidity would match that in your home.

To minimize changes in the wood, the best procedure is to store the wood for a while in the room in which the finished pieces made from it will be located. Thus, for example, if you had stored the wood for your table top in the dining room for a couple of weeks, and taken repeated readings with a meter until the moisture level of the wood had stabilized to match the level in your home, and then built the table, it probably would not have warped.

Beyond these precautions, it is a good idea to use woodworking designs in which the types of joints used will compensate for changes in humidity.

To sum up, the golden rules for avoiding this kind of problem are:
■ Make sure that you purchase only well-seasoned wood.
■ Try to balance the humidity of your workshop to that of your home.
■ Store the wood in the room in which the finished piece of furniture is to live.
■ Whenever possible, use designs and joints that allow for expansion and shrinkage.

See also: moisture / solution 2 / page 37

Groove

LEFT Easy-to-make wooden fasteners, screwed underneath the tabletop, both control and allow for movement.

Table top

Table apron

Screw

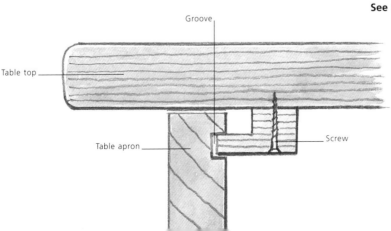

SELECTING THE RIGHT CUT AND ALTERNATING THE GRAIN

In many ways the behavior of a piece of furniture reflects the cut of wood from which the piece was made. For example, quarter-sawed hardwood (grain at right angles to the face) is less likely to shrink and cup than plain-sawed hardwood (grain rings curve from edge to edge across the face). While plain-sawed boards tend to shrink or expand across their width, quarter-sawn boards are more stable in their width and have the greatest change in thickness.

An extension of the problem has to do with the way in which the two cuts of wood—plain sawed and quarter sawed—distort as they dry out. While the rings as seen in the quarter-sawed board all look more or less the same length, the rings in the plain-sawed board show great variation in length. As there is an inherent inclination for the large rings to curve back from the small rings, it follows that while with quarter-sawed boards there is little or no movement, plain-sawed boards warp all over the place.

It may well be that the way you have arranged the boards is giving you trouble. No problem if you are using quarter-sawed boards, but if you are using plain-sawed boards, then you have a choice of arranging the boards so that the grain is alternately up and down, in which case the boards will cup up

ABOVE Tables made by "Stoneywell"—a collaboration between Neil Clarke and Ian Saville. Note the careful arrangement of the run of the grain.

and down, resulting in a wavy effect, or you can have the boards with all the hearts looking up, in which case the whole arrangement will arch up. So you can go for a rippled effect that is difficult to plane, or a bridge effect that is difficult—sometimes impossible—to hold down.

See also: understanding construction / solution 1 / page 18

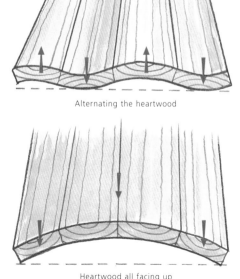

RIGHT Alternating heartwood up and down results in an overall wavy movement, while having heartwood all up results in a bridge-like movement of the whole piece.

Alternating the heartwood

Heartwood all facing up

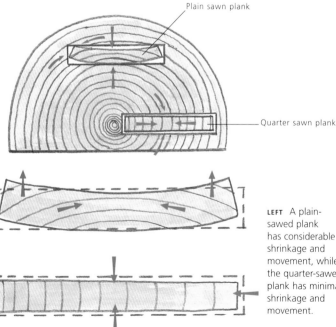

Plain sawn plank

Quarter sawn plank

LEFT A plain-sawed plank has considerable shrinkage and movement, while the quarter-sawed plank has minimal shrinkage and movement.

SLIDING SCREW BATTENS

Traditionally, country-style furniture—as with your plank table—has screwed and slotted battens across the underside of the top boards to help stiffen, support and hold the boards in place. The battens are

slotted and screwed to the underside of the structure, so that every board is held by at least one screw. When the changing humidity affects the boards and the whole structure starts to move, the boards are able to slide along the battens. In repairing your tabletop, such battens could be attached as a remedial treatment. The procedure is as follows:

1 First use some strong clamps to flatten out the table top, then set a couple of battens across the underside and mark them so that each board will be held by one or more screws. Make the battens about 2½ x 1½ in. Make the slots about ¼ in. long. Draw the position of the slots onto the two battens, and run three ¼ in. holes through for each slot.

2 Clean up the slots with a paring chisel. Use a fold of sandpaper to sand the holes to a smooth finish. It's important that the screw holes be clean, smooth and round-edged.

3 Select roundhead screws with washers to fit—long enough to go through the battens and about three-quarters of the way into the tabletop. The screws need to be a loose fit through the batten slots—with about 1 in. of smooth shank between the underside of the head and the start of the thread.

4 Sand the battens to a smooth finish and screw them in place on the underside of the table—with the screws all placed to the same end of the slots. If after a week or two the tabletop continues to move, then you have the option of fitting more battens, or battens of a larger section. If you must, you can further control the movement by making deep saw cuts on the underside of the table top—cuts that run the length of the boards.

See also: battens / solution 4 / page 87

table flap-up / solution 1/ page 85

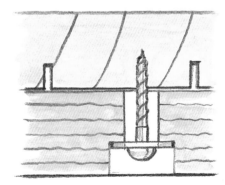

TOP LEFT An angled slot allows the wood to move both with and across the grain.

LEFT Some woodworkers prefer the screws set in oversized drilled holes with a slotted metal washer.

SLIDING DOVETAIL DADO

A more sophisticated solution than the sliding screwed batten is to use a sliding dovetail batten. The thinking behind such a dovetail is that while the planks can expand freely in width, they are held flat.

1 Measure and mark the position of the dovetail slot, cut the sides to about half the thickness of the tabletop with a fine-toothed back saw, and clear the scrap with a small plane.

2 Remove the front from a bullnose plane—so that you have the chisel option—and clear the slot to a uniform depth.

3 Use a paring chisel to undercut the sides of the slot to a dovetail section. We show a blind slot, but there is no reason why you can't cut it all the way through.

4 Use the chisel and plane to shape a sliding dovetail batten to fit. Aim for a tight push-fit.

5 Finally, tap the dovetail batten in dry. Do not use glue as it will defeat the whole object of the exercise, to allow the top to slide as it shrinks and expands.

See also: sliding dovetail / solution 3 / page 52

Sanding and Scraping

While sanding and scraping might not seem to be highly important in the greater scheme of things, there are times when deciding to scrape or sand, or how to improve surfaces that are less than perfect, can make the difference between success and failure. If you want answers, then read on.

29 I have just sanded an edge profile and it does not look very good. How can I fix it up? What is the best way of sanding such a profile?

Because an edge profile is noticeable, it should have a perfectly smooth finish.

solution 1

MAKING A BACKING BLOCK

A backing block is a block of wood shaped in reverse to fit the profile that you wish to sand, and used to support the sandpaper. It takes the guesswork out of sanding. So if you have a convex nosing, the block needs to have a concave shape that fits the nosing. Some woodworkers collect such blocks.

1 Transfer the profile to a small block of easy-to-carve wood, and shape it with a gouge and sandpaper. Try for a perfect fit.

2 Use double-sided sticky tape to cover the block profile with sandpaper. Use a steady, even stroke.

solution 2

MAKING A MINI DRUM SANDER FOR THE DRILL PRESS

If you enjoy woodturning, make yourself a shaped drum sander. It is a cylinder shaped sanding block, used in conjunction with a drill press.

1 Mount a block of easy-to-work wood in your lathe chuck, and turn it down to a cylinder. Turn a hollow in the middle that matches the edge that needs sanding. Turn a stem at one end so that it can be mounted in the drill chuck.

2 Use masking tape and double-sided sticky tape to cover the drum with sandpaper. Don't worry about wrinkles. Check for a good fit.

3 Finally, drill a hole up through the drum, and rig up a pivot jig to support the bottom of the drum. To sand, pass the workpiece by the spinning drum.

See also: drill press jig / solution 1 / page 120

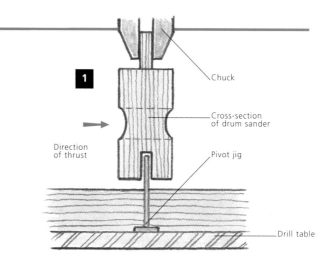

Chuck

Cross-section of drum sander

Direction of thrust

Pivot jig

Drill table

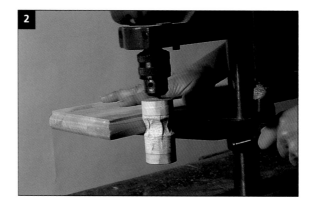

solution 3

MAKING A DISK PIVOT JIG

Suppose that you want to make a small, round plywood tabletop about 24 in. diameter, and you want to sand the edge to a fine finish before covering the edge with a strip of veneer. The edge needs to be perfectly smooth. Take the square sheet of plywood and establish the center by drawing crossed diagonals, and then draw and cut out the circle. Then take a 1 in. thick block of wood about 6 in. square, drill a ¼ in. diameter hole through the center, and mount it on the underside of the tabletop at the center.

Set a piece of ¼ in. diameter rod in your lathe's tool rest, and mount the whole works on the rod. Fit a sanding disk to the faceplate, and clamp a block to the bed so that the tabletop is level and the edge meets the sanding disk at right angles. You should be able to rotate the tabletop against the disk. All you do now is switch on the lathe and slowly pivot the top until the edge is sanded to your satisfaction.

See also: jigs / solutions 1–10 / pages 120–5

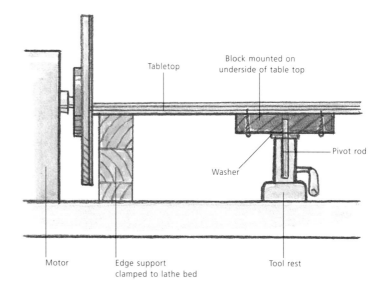

Tabletop

Block mounted on underside of table top

Pivot rod

Washer

Motor

Edge support clamped to lathe bed

Tool rest

ABOVE Switch on the lathe, and hand turn the tabletop so that the edge comes into contact with the sanding disc

30 I just finished making a table. Unfortunately I dropped my hand plane on it, and now there is a sizable dent in the surface. How can I repair it?

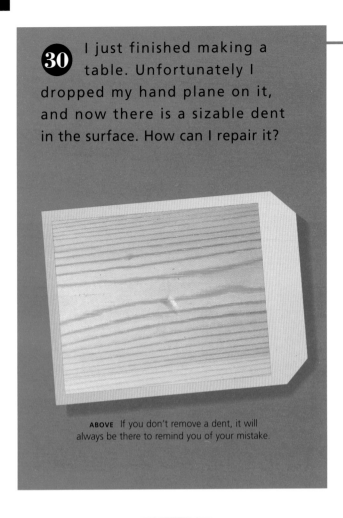

ABOVE If you don't remove a dent, it will always be there to remind you of your mistake.

solution 1

STEAMING

One way of removing a dent in an unfinished surface is to raise it with steam.

1 Dab water into the dent with a brush and let it soak in for a couple of minutes.

2 Then, having first tested the procedure on a piece of scrap wood, use a laundry iron to apply heat—so that the wood fibers swell and realign. Be careful not to scorch the wood. If the wood is sticky or resinous, put a damp cloth between the wood and the iron.

See also: steam bending / solution 3 / page 90

solution 2

CLEAR FILLER

If the dent is in a piece that has been finished with clear varnish, lacquer or other finish, then another solution is to fill the dent with the same finish.

1 Wipe the surface with a cloth dampened with mineral spirits, and let it dry.

2 Use a small watercolor brush to drip a very small drop of finish into the dent. Wait for the drop to dry and then repeat until the dent is flush. Don't try to fill it up in one pass.

3 Use a soft cloth to burnish the repaired surface.

See also: varnish glaze / solution 3 / page 101

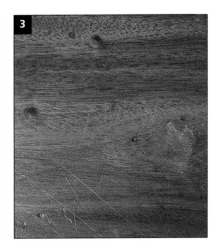

solution 3

WAX FILLER

Wax fillers are crayon-like sticks of hard wax that are used to repair dents and scratches that occur after a surface has been finished. They come in various shapes, sizes, colors and forms. Depending upon the type—meaning consistency—they can be melted together for a color match and then applied, or they can be mixed as a paste and then applied, or they can be kneaded like a putty, or they can be melted straight into the dent, and so on.

I know a woodworker who always carries wax fillers around in his toolbox. The idea is that when he visits homes to deliver or repair furniture, he can please clients by instantly mending the dents and scratches that most people have on a best table or other piece. The clients are happy, and he gets the pleasure of a job well done.

1 Study the dent and decide on the best color match. If you want a perfect color match, it might be a good idea to turn the table over and try it out on an area hidden from view.

2 Use a small sliver of wood to work the wax into the dent. If you are using hard wax, and the hole is deep, it's a good idea to use a hot knife or soldering iron to melt and puddle the wax into place.

3 Use a cotton cloth to burnish the wax. If need be, scrape off the excess wax with the edge of a straight-bladed knife.

See also: beeswax / solution 4 / page 99

solution 4

VENEER PATCH

Even if your table surface is veneered, you may be able to steam out a dent in the same way as described above for solid wood. If steaming does not work—the substrate remains dented—you can cut in a patch of matching veneer. Hold the new piece of veneer over the dented area so that the grain is aligned and the light catches it in the same way. With dark veneers, matching is even easier. Cut through both veneers while holding the patch in this position. Very tough wood may require a second cut. Make the patch as small as possible, but shape it to look natural.

See also: veneer / solution 3 / page 45

LEFT If you take time carefully matching grain—its direction, color and character—a veneered surface can be patched to perfection.

Glues and Clamps

Many woodworking beginners spend hours cutting joints to perfection, and then cancel out all their effort by careless gluing and clamping. Though with gluing and clamping you usually have only one chance to get it right, there are ways of fixing mistakes. Here we show you how.

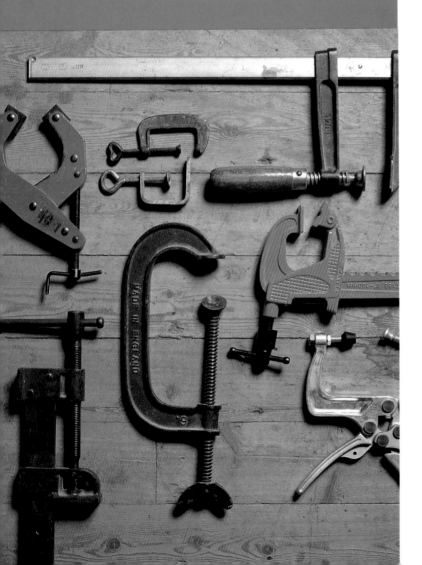

31 I have a beautiful chair—all glued together. But now that the glue has set, I find that the frame is misaligned! How can I correct the problem?

ABOVE If the legs are badly out of line, they must be redone.

solution 1

USING BAR CLAMPS

Though in the context of clamping a chair, bar clamps are for the most part not easy to use—they are stiff and heavy—you can use them if you take trouble with the setup, and get a friend to help.

1 You need two strong boards—one to put the chair on, and one on top of the chair seat. Have your clamps open to the right width and ready, and make sure that all the equipment you need is conveniently at hand. Start by having a dry trial run.

2 Now glue the joints and put the chair together, and get a friend to help you set the clamps in place. Spend time checking with a measure and square until the structure seems symmetrical, and then carefully tighten the clamps. If the chair is not itself symmetrical—and most simple wooden chairs are not—then check by eye and adjust for what looks best.

See also: clamps / solution 2 / page 79
bar clamps / solution 3 / page 81

solution 2

STEAMING AND DISASSEMBLING

The wonderful thing about using hot hide glue, is the fact that it is so user-friendly. Okay… so it smells a wee bit, but once you get to know its positive attributes, the smell will be as nothing—like roses even! Its easy to prepare, it has a high open time, it is sandable, it fills gaps, it bonds to oily wood, it can be cleaned up with water, it is low cost, it is non-toxic, and best of all it is totally reversible. If you don't like the glue-up, you simple soften the glue with steam and start over.

1 Take your steamer and set to work softening the glue. I have found that a wallpaper steamer fitted with a fine-point nozzle works best. Direct the full force of the steam on and in the joints. When you feel the joints begin to move, then use a rubber-headed mallet to knock and ease the structure apart. Be warned: if you try to twist and bend the chair apart before the glue has softened, you risk breaking the wood. Be patient, and be generous with the steam.

2 Before disassembly, label the component parts with a pencil so that you know precisely what goes

where and how. Spend time scraping off all the glue from the mortises and the ends of the rails. Finally, do a dry run trial to make sure that you know the right order of reassembly.

See also: gluing / solution 1 / page 30

USING A ROPE CLAMP

One of the best ways of clamping up a chair—or any other structure that is irregular—is to use a band clamp. A band clamp consists of a length of strong fabric, 2 in. wide, and a metal clamp at one end, through which the other end threads. If one is not available, you can use the following emergency procedure.

1 Wrap the rope or webbing several times from leg to leg across the diagonal, knot off, pass the stick through the loop, and wind up until the twisting takes up the slack and begins to pull everything together. Compare diagonals until they more or less match up, and then tie the stick so that it stays put.

2 The rope and stick method is great for pulling the legs onto the stretchers. Just about the only thing that you have to watch out for is that you don't overdo the winding and break the chair. That said, be careful that the stick doesn't unwind all of a rush and strike you. It is a good idea to wear goggles.

See also: bar clamps / solution 1 / page 74

MAKING CORNER CLAMPS

A common problem often crops up when clamping chairs that have the back legs running up to form posts—how to pull the post into the seat without damaging one or both members, and without pulling the seat frame askew. A simple answer—make a set of clamping blocks to fit the chair. The procedure is to cut two blocks, one to fit on the outside of the chair post, and the other to fit inside the seat frame. It's fairly easy and straightforward, so long as you bear in mind that the inside-seat block must be no larger than the corner angle of the seat frame. If you get them right, the blocks will not only pull the post and the seat together, they will also ensure that the frame is correctly angled.

See also: joints / solution 1 / page 26

RIGHT Cut v-shaped blocks of wood that will grip the back legs of the chair enabling you to do up the clamps without them slipping. These blocks also stop the chair from being damaged and exert the force of the clamps in the right direction.

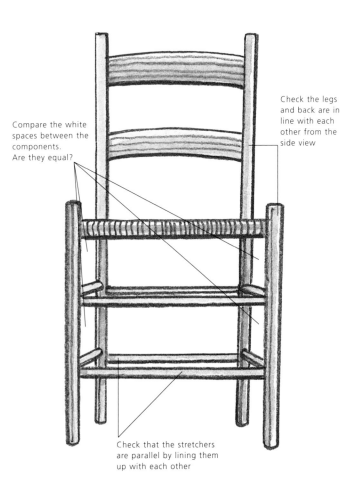

Check the legs and back are in line with each other from the side view

Compare the white spaces between the components. Are they equal?

Check that the stretchers are parallel by lining them up with each other

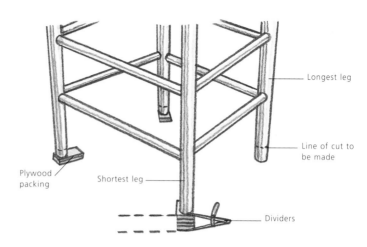

ABOVE Match up all the legs to the one that is shortest.

LEVELING CHAIR LEGS

One problem with making a chair is how to level the legs so that all four stand firm and sit on the floor without rocking. I remember when I first started woodworking, I wanted to saw the legs of an old chair down so that it was low, like a stool. I cut all four, but it rocked a little, so I trimmed off more from another leg, and continued until I wound up with something that was only about 9 in. off the floor. A good lesson learned, I suppose. Because it's almost impossible to make a chair that stands without rocking at the first try, it's a good idea to start out by making the legs slightly longer and then cutting back. I know of one chairmaker who makes all his Windsor chair legs about 3 in. longer than they need to be, so he can trim them as needed.

1 Set your chair on a level surface. Then put a spirit level on the seat and proceed to shim the legs with thin pieces of scrap—I use thin pieces of plywood—until the spirit bubble shows it is level from front to back and from side to side.

2 Take a pair of dividers and use them to measure from the bottom of the shortest leg—meaning the leg with the greatest amount of shim—to the floor.

3 Use the dividers to step or scribe this distance off on the other three legs. It's got to be right the first time around, so if you have any doubts, stop and reconsider.

4 Use a fine-bladed saw to cut all the legs to the same length. Finally, smooth the cut ends with sandpaper and the job is done.

See also: dimensions / solution 1 / page 21

CHECKING FOR SQUARE

Once the whole chair frame has been glued and clamped together, then you need to test that the whole structure is true and symmetrical. One way is to use a tape rule or a long piece of scrap to go over the chair making sure that like diagonals are equal. For example, the diagonals across the bottoms of the legs need to be the same, and the diagonals across the stretcher joints, and so on. Don't take this to an extreme, because chairs are by their very nature usually less than symmetrical, but at least make sure that the chair is going to stand level and the structure looks good to your eye. A good test is to stand the chair on a table so that the seat is at eye level and then to take a sighting from front-center through to the back, and compare the shape of the spaces in and around the various members.

LEFT Position the chair so that you can see it from the front, with the seat at eye level, and then compare the various spaces between the parts.

32 I am ready to start making slab seats for Windsor chairs—and all but one of my clamps are being used on another job. What can I do?

RUBBED JOINTS

Rubbed joints are a traditional way to joint several narrow boards together without clamps—if you use hot hide glue. Heat the glue until it is thin in consistency, then brush it on mating edges and rub the two boards together until they resist. Repeat for each board. The resulting slab is stood on edge and leaned against an inclined batten. This technique should be limited to boards no longer than 4 ft. Hot hide glue is perfect for building up slabs for Windsor chairs—it has plenty of grip, it is strong and durable, and the whole procedure can be managed without the need for clamps.

1 Arrange the boards for best fit, and mark the arrangement so that you know the order. Clamp the first board in a vise, brush glue on the mating edges, set the second board edge-to-edge with the first, and slide it left and right until it grips. As soon as you have a good fit, brush glue on the next pair of edges.

2 Be sure always to keep your hands at the ends, with the thumbs across the joint so that you can feel it if the joint comes apart.

3 Be generous with the glue, especially at the ends. If you feel the glue begin to get thick or in any way lumpy, put the glue pot back on the heater.

4 At the end, check the stack of boards for squareness, and then stand the slab on edge and against a leaning batten so that it is held by its own weight.

See also: gluing / solution 1 / page 40

clamps / solution 1 / page 74

solution 2

CROSS-SCREW CLAMPS

If you prefer to use some other adhesive, and you are prepared for slightly more end-of-slab scrap, you can use the one-clamp-and-screws method. All you do is glue, lightly clamp at the center, drive in the screws across the ends, remove the clamp and go on to the next board.

1 After having glued in much the same way as already described, and clamped the boards at the center—not too tightly—then drill at an angle across the joint and drive in a long screw.

2 Run second screws at an angle across the first, so that you can feel the boards being drawn up. If you are working on a whole stack of slabs, then it's a good idea to use a power screwdriver.

See also: clamps / solution 1 / page 74

solution 3

USING DOGS

Using pinch dogs is another traditional solution for clamping three or four boards. They are easy to use, they are low in cost, they can be used with slow-cure glue, and they can be used without the need for a complex setup. You need a pinch dog to bridge each end joint—four boards equals six dogs.

1 Spread adhesive on the edges of the boards and lightly clamp the whole works in the center with your one free clamp.

2 Bridge a dog across each joint, one at a time, and tap it home. If all goes well, the dogs will clench the boards to the extent that the center clamp falls away of its own accord.

33 I glued up a bed end, and it is out of square. Why did this happen? How can I disassemble it and make sure this doesn't happen again?

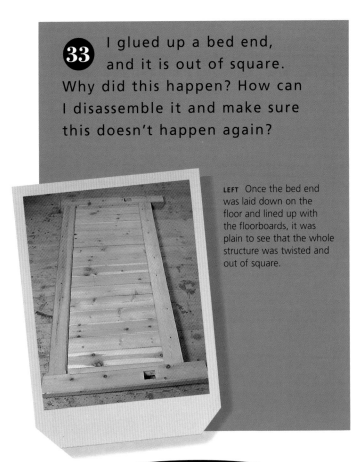

LEFT Once the bed end was laid down on the floor and lined up with the floorboards, it was plain to see that the whole structure was twisted and out of square.

---

solution 1

CHECKING JOINTS AND REGLUING THE FRAME

First, lay the bed end flat on a floor and study it to pinpoint the problem. If the floor has a pattern of tiles or floorboards, then so much the better. Align the bed end with an edge line of tiles or floorboards to see the way it is twisted, and use a square to check the corners.

With respect to the bed end pictured, it is plain to see that the overall structure is reasonably square, but a twist is revealed by the near right corner's being off the floor. This was caused in the main by the joint at that corner being slightly askew and a bit sloppy and slack. On consideration, I decided that an additional vertical member in the middle would have kept things straight.

After thinking it over, we decided that the best course of action was to disassemble the bed end, clean up the joints, redowel them, fill in the loose joints with shims, and then to compensate for the twist by pulling the whole assembly square and reclamping it before regluing it.

See also: good joints / solution 4 / page 32

---

solution 2

DRILLING OUT THE DOWELS AND STEAMING

Though drilling out the dowels and steaming is pretty straightforward, it does need to be managed with care. This procedure also works with PVA glue.

1 Select two drill bits, one about $\frac{1}{8}$-in. diameter for the pilot holes and the other one the same diameter as the dowels. If the dowels are blind at the bottom end, put a piece of masking tape around the bits as a depth gauge. Drill pilot holes at dead center in the dowel ends, and then use the dowel-size bit to drill out the dowels.

2 Fire up your steamer and aim the fine-point nozzle directly in the holes. This will heat up the joint and loosen the glue so that the joint can be pulled apart.

See also: steaming / solution 2/ page 75

solution 3

REVERSE CLAMPING

If the joints are tight and you are worried that knocking the joint apart with a mallet will twist or break the joint, then use a bar clamp or similar clamp with a screw action and separate heads, and reverse the main head so that the clamp can be used to push the joint apart rather than clamp it.

1 Unwind the head of the clamp from the bar and reverse it so that the screw thread pushes it outward. Set the clamp in place across the ends of the frame, with pieces of scrap wood between the heads and the workpiece to protect the faces of the workpiece. Mounting separate-head clamps on your own wood batten might be a good idea, because you can more easily make up an arrangement to suit the design of the job in hand. Get a helper to set up another reversed clamp on the other side of the frame. After the joint is well steamed, slowly wind out the clamps in order to ease the frame apart.

2 After you have taken the frame completely apart, spend some time with a chisel and a scraper working on the pieces to make sure that all mating faces of the joints are clean and free from glue. Pay particular attention to the corners of the tenon.

See also: bar clamps / solution 1 / page 74

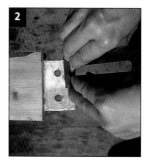

solution 4

SQUARING UP THE FRAME

While there are all sorts of ways to use clamps to pull a frame square, it's really only a matter of experimenting with the clamps until the structure is square and there is a minimum of twist. This might involve weighing down corners of the frame, clamping the frame to a bench, placing the clamps across the corners, and so on. Be sure to do this squaring up and clamping before actually applying the glue, of course.

1 Push the frame together dry, and place it on a level surface. Then play around with the clamps until the whole piece comes together correctly and squarely. Use a square to check the angles at the corners, measure from the floor/bench to check twist, measure diagonals, and so on.

2 If the frame is still twisted, clamp one end to the bench and add a weight at the other. Look closely at the joints to see if they have opened up so much as to need shims or wedges. When you have squared up the frame, with no twist or buckle, take note of the clamping arrangement, disassemble the whole works, and glue and reclamp. Don't forget to make final checks before the glue dries.

See also: shims / solution 1 / page 30

ABOVE Use clamps, wedges and weights to push and pull the structure square.

BELOW Adjust and modify the clamps to square up the frame.

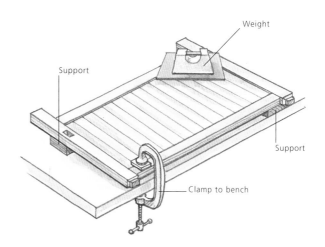

Weight

Support

Support

Clamp to bench

34 I have assembled a small box. Glue dribbles have ruined the surface. Can I repair the damage? How can I avoid the problem in the future?

ABOVE If you think this is a bad dribble … !

solution 1

DISASSEMBLE AND SCRAPE

If you have used traditional hot hide glue, it is reversible. The newer adhesives and cements can only be removed with tricky and difficult solvents. A hot hide glue joint can be fairly easily steamed apart and the glue residue scraped off. It requires effort and perseverance, but it can be done.

1 Steam the joints until the glue becomes soft and then gently ease the box apart. Use a warm knife or scraper to remove the bulk of the glue. Work both with and across the grain. Wipe the scraped glue off onto a piece of scrap wood—if you try to use tissue or newspaper to clean the scraping tool, you will finish up with a sticky mess.

2 Spend time carefully removing all traces of the glue from inside the joint. If the joint is small, you might try wiping the glue out with a fine-point brush and hot water.

3 When you have removed as much of the warm glue as possible, let the remainder cool and set, and then sand it off with a block and sandpaper.

See also: glues / solution 1 / page 40

solution 2

SURFACE PREPARATION

While it is of course vital that you should have a dry trial assembly before you apply any glue—all clamps and other materials close at hand and ready—it is equally important that the mating surfaces of the wood be properly prepared. Ideally, gluing should occur as soon as possible after the wood has been worked. If there has been a long delay, spend some time wiping the pieces clean of dust and other debris. If you are gluing together a joint mostly made up of end grain, it's a good idea to seal the grain before gluing. I usually seal the end grain with a very thin mix of hot water and hide glue. I paint the diluted glue on and in the joint, and then glue and clamp as usual.

See also: sanding / solution 2 / page 95

solution 3

HOW TO MINIMIZE GLUING PROBLEMS

I was once told that the three most important rules for successful gluing are careful preparation, careful preparation, and careful preparation! Though the following procedure may seem a bit finicky, it is the best way to keep glue off finished surfaces.

1 After doing a trial dry assembly so that you know precisely what goes where and how, use low-tack masking tape to cover all the areas outside the joint that you want free from glue.

2 Use a small fine-point brush to apply glue carefully to all mating surfaces.

3 Put the piece together, check for alignment and squareness, and then clamp.

4 Wait until the glue is set, then peel away the tape and scrape the surfaces to a fine finish.

See also: assembly order / solution 6 / page 20

Construction

For many woodworkers, one joy of woodworking is how to save the day in a clever way. So if you have done something that did not work out, or you are fast running out of ideas to bring a project to a happy conclusion, then one of the following solutions may be what you are looking for.

 35 I am making a chair that has round, tapered spindles. My lathe is out of action—how can I make the spindles without using a lathe?

solution 1

USING A DRAWKNIFE

A good way around this problem is to go back to handtool work.

1 Take a length of knot-free square-section wood—length and section size to suit your design—establish the end centers by drawing crossed diagonals, and mark the ends with circles. Mark in the halfway point along the length.

2 Secure the wood in the vise so that one end is looking up at you, and shave off the corner. Work with your elbows held tight to your waist and with the bevel side of the blade facing up.

3 The procedure is shave and turn, shave and turn—turning the wood in the vise and carving the wood down to match the round end section. When you have shaved one end, then do the same procedure for the other end.

4 Finally, sand the spindle smooth with sandpaper.

WORKING WITH A KNIFE AND SPOKESHAVE

If you don't own a drawknife, then use a good, sharp knife and a spokeshave—a spokeshave is designed for shaving spokes, which are much like spindles.

1 Prepare and mark the wood as described left and set to work shaving with the knife. The main difference this time is that you are cutting away from your body, rather than towards it. Take off the bulk of the scrap wood with broad strokes.

2 When you have roughed out the shape, change the stroke to a more controlled thumb-pushing stroke, with the thumb of one hand supplying extra leverage by pushing on the back of the blade.

3 Work both ends as described, and then continue to shave and pare with the knife. If you do not want to finish with the knife, you can do the final work with the spokeshave. Ideally you need to use a round-soled shave—meaning one designed specifically for working hollows. If you own a set of wooden spokeshaves, then you have the perfect tools for the job!

36 My workshop is short of space. I need an easily made fold-up table for gluing. Have you any ideas?

FOLDING WALL TABLE

This table has a top that lifts up to rest on a pair of swing-out bracket hinges. It can be made to fit into a recess or fixed against a wall. The brackets can be hinged to the side pieces or made with drop pins. The framing needs to be secured strongly to the wall. One advantage of this design is that the space above the table can be used for other things—shelves, a pegboard, a window, or whatever.

See also: table top / solution 3 / page 68

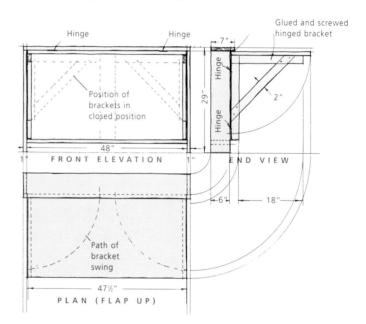

FOLDING WALL TABLE CUTTING LIST

- Top shelf board—50 x 7 x 1 inch, 1 piece.
- Side boards— 28 x 6 x 1 inch, 2 pieces.
- Table flap—47½ x 22 x 1 inch, 1 piece of plywood.
- Kick board—48 x 6 x 1 inch, 1 piece.
- Bracket top arm—18 x 2 x 1 inch, 2 pieces.
- Bracket vertical—24 x 2 x 1 inch, 2 pieces.
- Bracket diagonal—28 x 2 x 1 inch, 2 pieces.
- Hinges—6

All sizes approximate—modify to suit your needs

solution 2

NORWEGIAN KLAPPBORD

This design draws its inspiration from a traditional Norwegian folding wall table known as a "klappbord." Such a table was a regular fixture in most mid-nineteenth century Norwegian-American homes. When the table is not in use, it is flipped up against the wall, where the fancy underside becomes a decorative feature. The good thing about this table is that you can use the floor space for other items. If you want to go for a more functional design, you can skip the fretting, and use metal hinges.

See also: alternating grain / solution 2/ page 67

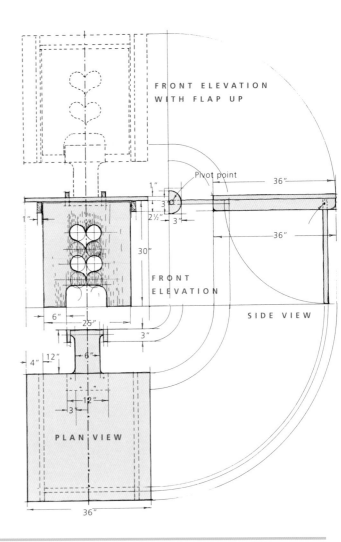

FRONT ELEVATION WITH FLAP UP

Pivot point

FRONT ELEVATION

SIDE VIEW

PLAN VIEW

NORWEGIAN KLAPPBORD CUTTING LIST
• Table flap—36 x 36 x 1 inch, 1 piece.
• Flap leg—29½ x 25 x 1 inch, 1 piece.
• Hinge board—17 x 12 x 1 inch, 1 piece.
• Hinge plates—6 x 3 x 1 inch, 2 pieces.
• Table bearers—36 x 3 x 1 inch, 2 pieces.
All sizes approximate—modify to suit your needs

solution 3

SAWHORSE TABLE

This is an easy-to-make table—no construction required at all, just two sawhorses and a sheet of ¾ in. plywood for the top. The horses can be used by themselves for other tasks—sawing, planing, working outside, and so on. When you need a table, you simply set the plywood sheet on the sawhorses and you are ready to go. I tend to use just about everything from a sheet of plywood to planks for the tabletop, depending on the task at hand.

See also: workshop / solution 3 / page 12

FRONT ELEVATION

SIDE VIEW

PLAN VIEW

JOINT DETAIL

SAWHORSE TABLE CUTTING LIST
• Top beam—33 x 4 x 3 inch, 1 piece.
• Leg—24 x 3 x 3 inch, 4 pieces.
• End underbeam stretcher—10 x 4 x 1 inch, 2 pieces.
• End bottom stretcher— 16 x 3 x 1 inch, 2 pieces.
• Front stretcher—30 x 3 x 1 inch, 2 pieces.
All sizes approximate—modify to suit your needs

solution 4

GATELEG TABLE

Gateleg tables in one form or another have been around for hundreds of years. They are a good choice for a workshop, because the gates, when opened out to become legs, give the top solid support—weight is transferred directly down the legs to the floor, rather than putting strain on hinges. The maximum length of the leaf—and therefore the length of the top—is governed by the height of the table. The design shown has two leaves, which make a tabletop double the table height in length. The width depends on the width of the leg frames. As dining tables, gateleg tables usually have fancy joints and hinges, but a workshop version can be made with steel strap-type hinges. My workshop gateleg table has been designed to use sheets of 3/4-in plywood, so that you can have it done and in use in the shortest possible time, but there is no reason why you can't modify the design and frame the gates.

If you like this table, but two leaves would make it too big, you can change the design so that it only has a single leaf, with what is now the central section a frame or shelf fixed to the wall. If you are worried about the leaves or gates twisting, you can use battens to stiffen the design. I think that the main plus of a gateleg table is strength.

See also: battens / solution 3 / page 68

table flap up / solution 1 / page 85

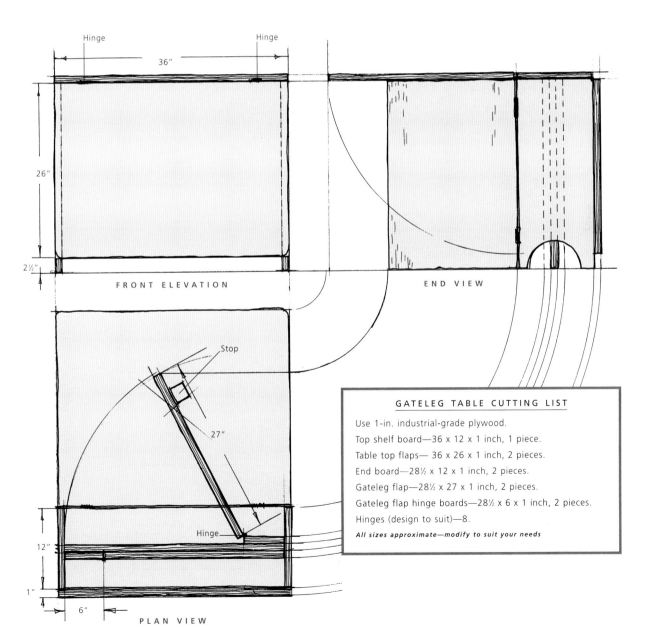

Hinge   Hinge

36"

26"

2½"

FRONT ELEVATION   END VIEW

Stop

27"

Hinge

12"

1"

6"

PLAN VIEW

GATELEG TABLE CUTTING LIST

Use 1-in. industrial-grade plywood.
Top shelf board—36 x 12 x 1 inch, 1 piece.
Table top flaps— 36 x 26 x 1 inch, 2 pieces.
End board—28½ x 12 x 1 inch, 2 pieces.
Gateleg flap—28½ x 27 x 1 inch, 2 pieces.
Gateleg flap hinge boards—28½ x 6 x 1 inch, 2 pieces.
Hinges (design to suit)—8.
All sizes approximate—modify to suit your needs

37 I am making curved chair arms in sawn sections and they are not coming out right. I need a technique for doing it correctly. Have you any ideas? How do I produce the right curves?

JOINTING AND CARVING CURVES

If you cut a full curve from a single board, there will be two or more points around the curve where the grain is at right angles and so short that the curve will fracture across it. If you look at traditional chairs, you will see that this problem was traditionally overcome by first building the curves up from short, straight-grained sections overlapped and doweled together, then carved and sculpted to shape. While this technique can work, it sometimes results in cracked joints from the weight of a person sitting in the chair. To correct this, the arms and backs of some of these segmented chairs were built up in sandwiched layers with the vulnerable joints staggered. In using this approach, it is best to join the staggered pieces with glue plus dowels inserted from the underside.

See also: cutting curves / solution 9/ page 115

draw knife / solution 1 / page 84

ABOVE If you try to cut a curve from one piece of wood, there will be weak areas of short grain as shown by the crosses.

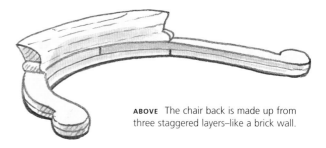

ABOVE The chair back is made up from three staggered layers–like a brick wall.

RIGHT A classic smoker's chair with a laminated bow back.

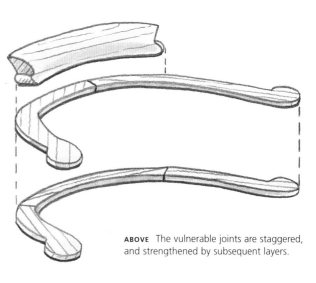

ABOVE The vulnerable joints are staggered, and strengthened by subsequent layers.

LAMINATING CURVES

Curves can be built up by gluing thin strips or laminations of wood into a sandwich and clamping it in a former. Ideally, the laminations should be about ⅛ in. thick and made from a straight-grained wood like beech, birch, spruce or ash. When the curved bundle is removed from the former after the glue dries, the various layers are locked in place and the shape holds.

1 Use your fractured curve or a template of it as a master. Transfer the shape to the wood that you are going to use for the former. Cut the shape out on the band saw, or with a bow saw. Bear in mind that the end product is only going to be as good as the shape of the former.

2 Spend time getting yourself organized, setting out all the tools and materials so that they are close at hand. Have a practice run. Decide where the actual gluing is going to take place. Consider whether or not you need a friend to help.

3 Cut the ⅛ in. laminations to size. Allow a good amount at each end for scrap. Though most laminations can be glued up without keying—especially if they have just been cut—it's a good idea with wood that has been lying around to key the mating faces with the edge of an old saw.

4 Brush the glue on both sides of the wood.

5 Immediately put the glued "sandwich" in the former and clamp it tight—so that the glue oozes out.

6 When dried, take the sandwich out of the former, trim off the waste ends—leaving some extra for final finishing and fitting—and begin carving.

See also: laminating / solution 2 / page 29

ABOVE A prototype for a steambent chair. The back is laminated from 15 or so 2 inch wide strips of beech constructional veneer. The whole bundle of strips were covered with glue then bent and clamped around a light-bulb shaped former. To make the back comfortable, it also curved from the side elevation. A jigsaw was used to cut the second curve out of the depth of the laminated shape. Surforms and rasps were used to create the final tapering circular section.

STEAMBENDING

If you take a longbow and bend it, the moment you let go it will spring back to its former shape. If you go on bending, there will come a time when the fibers will tear and part. But if you first heat the bow with steam or by soaking it in hot water, the fibers will relax so that it can be more easily bent—and if the bent bow is held until it is cold, it will be locked in the new shape.

While hot water and steam work equally well, it is more practical to use steam. The easiest procedure is to build a steamer box out of plywood to suit the length of wood that you plan to steam. For example, to steam a board 6 x 1 in. x 6 ft, you would need a box 8 x 4 in. x 6½ ft. The extra space allows room for the steam to circulate. The box needs an inlet hole at one end and a vent and drain at the other. It's a good idea to wrap insulation around the box, and then cover the whole works with silver foil.

The water is heated up and piped into the steamer box. You need to allow about 1 hr steaming time for every 1-in. thickness of wood. Once the wood has been steamed, take it promptly from the box, bend it around the former, and then clamp it in place until it is cold. Seasoned wood is difficult to bend, and green wood is easy to bend but prone to tearing, so half-seasoned wood with about 20–25% water is ideal for steambending.

The trick is being able to handle the hot wood and to control the bending. A workpiece should be bent promptly after heating, before it has a chance to cool down. Curves should be slightly overbent to allow for a small amount of later relaxing and unbending.

One way to control bending is to use a strap of thin stainless spring steel, so that when the wood has been bent, the steel is on the outside face of the curve. This not only makes it easier to handle and bend the wood, but the steel strap on the convex face helps to prevent the wood fibers from tearing out. I have found that large planks can be more easily bent if I use extension handles or a winch to increase the leverage—similar to a windlass of the kind used to trim the sails on a large boat.

See also: steaming / solution 2 / page 75

LEFT A classic chair designed in the nineteenth century by the German craftsman Michael Thonet. Its beautiful, fluid shape was produced almost entirely by steambending.

LEFT A classic Windsor chair form made by the English manufacturer Ercol. Note the way the back and arms are created from a single length of steambent wood.

RIGHT An experimental side chair. This was made by steam-bending a single plank of green ash. It is incredibly strong and good fun to sit on!

ABOVE Whole planks can be successfully steambent. The technique requires a lot of effort. This two-piece jig, one piece for each curve, has stainless steel sheets to control the movement.

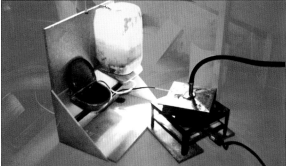

ABOVE The steamer consists of a water supply, a boiler, and a wooden chest to collect the steam.

ABOVE The workpiece is secured in a jig consisting of a stainless-steel sheet and wooden blocks.

ABOVE Three people using a simple jig to steambend a stool.

ABOVE With some designs requiring the curves to change direction as in an S, the jig needs to be designed so that the workpiece can be wrapped around the forming blocks.

RIGHT After steaming, a bend should be held for a couple of days in a de-humidifying cabinet while it sets.

38 I have just built a cabinet with a hinge-down lid. The hinges are too weak, and the lid is likely to fold back on itself and break off. What can I do?

solution 1

USING LARGER HINGES

Remove the small hinges. Buy the best solid brass hinges—not brassed or pressed—and mark and recut the recesses to fit.

1 Place the new hinges over the old recesses so that the pin is perfectly centered with the edge. Score around the flap with the point of a knife. Set a gauge to the thickness of the flap and run a line along the edge of the wood.

2 Cut the recesses out with a bevel-edged paring chisel. Set the chisel to the scrap side of the scored line and cut in to the depth of the hinge flap. Divide the length of the scrap with two more down cuts. Carefully pare away the scrap so the recess fits the new hinge.

See also: dovetail hinge / solution 1 / page 28

solution 2

LID STAYS WITH DROP BRAKES

There are all kinds of lid and door stays on the market—some so complex that you need to be a true master craftsman to know how to install one properly—so spend time choosing the right kind of drop brake stay to suit your particular piece.

1 After you have carefully studied your chosen stay and all the associated instructional paperwork —and this isn't easy when it appears to have been written in some language resembling Serbo-Croat—spend a few moments building a mockup. This need not be anything very sophisticated, just a few scrap pieces of wood. The hope is, of course, that all your experimental holes will appear in the mockup and none, or far fewer, in the workpiece.

2 Finally, when you have worked out all the false starts and stops on the mockup and you are absolutely clear in your own mind as to how the stay should be attached, screw it in place. Even after carefully following my own advice, I still wound up redoing the job to change the angle!

solution 3

LIFT-UP LOCKING STAY WITH BUFFER

Lift-up locking stays with buffers are surface-mounted mechanisms that allow you to lift up the lid and lock it in position—and then by lifting the lid slightly further, you can let the lid down. If you let go of the lid, the buffer acts as a brake. While I'm personally not keen on fittings of this type—mainly because they are too sophisticated—this particular mechanism might be just what you are looking for to help keep your lid safe.

It is advisable to install this device in the same way as is done with the chest stay described above—using a mockup and experimenting with it—because the positioning is very specific, making it a good deal more complicated than the lid stay. To make matters more interesting, while the manufacturer's directions are written in German, French and English, and the measurements in metric, the how-to-install-it illustrations are really not adequate for the purpose!

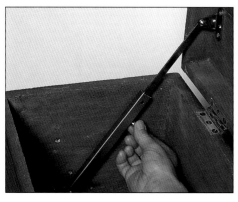

LEFT Avoid mistakes by building a mockup to establish how the stay needs to be positioned.

LEFT Screw the stay in place and adjust the braking mechanism to allow the lid to drift down.

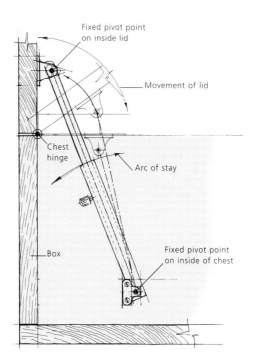

Fixed pivot point on inside lid

Movement of lid

Chest hinge

Arc of stay

Box

Fixed pivot point on inside of chest

ABOVE While this particular type of stay is designed to allow the lid to fall at a controlled pace, installing it is a bit tricky.

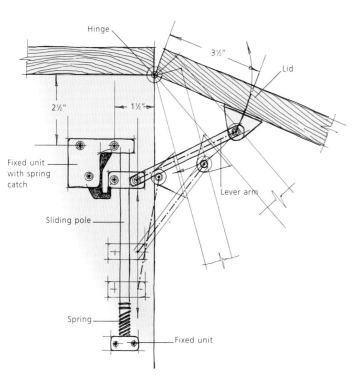

Hinge

3½"

Lid

2½"

1½"

Fixed unit with spring catch

Lever arm

Sliding pole

Spring

Fixed unit

ABOVE Stays like this are designed to lift up and lock. If the cupboard flap falls down by accident, the spring acts as a buffer and slows the fall.

ABOVE Build a mockup to work out how the lift-up-and-lock mechanism works. Establish the precise positioning.

Wood Finishing

Woodworking projects are mainly judged by their finish, yet probably more projects are spoiled at the finishing stage than anywhere else along the line. The good news is that a bad finish can be corrected in almost less time than it takes to tell how to do it.

39 My lacquered finish is a mess! What am I doing wrong? What now?

ABOVE A dripping curtain of dry lacquer is an embarrassment, as well as being ugly.

solution 1

FILLING THE GRAIN

It is possible that your wood is open-grained, and needs to be filled before lacquering. There are all kinds of fillers on the market, in a whole range of colors and recipes. After using a cabinet-scraper to remove the lacquer, swab a generous amount of your chosen color-matched filler on the surface, and use a piece of lint-free cloth to work it into the grain. Rub with a circular motion and wipe off the excess across the grain. Finally, sand the dry filler with a fine-grade sandpaper.

See also grain / solution 3 / page 98

ABOVE Wipe a generous amount of filler into the grain, and then wipe the excess off across the run of the grain.

solution 2

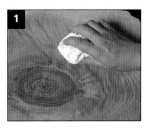
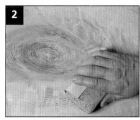

SUPER-FINE FINISHING

Super-fine finishing involves using a scraper followed up by the use of garnet and/or flour paper.

1 Highlight the grain by wiping the surface with mineral spirits, so that you get an idea of the pattern of the grain.

2 Wrap your chosen abrasive paper around a block and sand in the direction of the grain.

3 If the grain swirls, it would be advisable to use a scraper rather than an abrasive paper, to avoid scratching the surface across the grain.

4 Some woodworkers consider that a properly burred scraper is the best tool for creating a perfectly smooth surface in any case—much better than abrasive paper, no matter what the grain pattern!

See also: surface preparation / solution 2 / page 83

---

solution 3

THE SPRAYING ENVIRONMENT

If you are using a spray gun to apply lacquer, then not only is it vital that the spraying area be clean from dust and debris, but more than that, you need to be working in a safe environment. One of the simplest solutions is to build yourself a spray booth in the corner of the workshop.

All you need is a three-sided booth, with a door on the fourth side, a good-sized extractor fan in the back wall that vents to the open air, plenty of light, and a surface with a turntable. The lights must be explosion proof, as must the extractor fan motor. Cover the hole with several layers of fine cotton gauze so that as the spray mist is drawn through the fan the gauze catches all the solids. To prevent the fan from drawing dust and dirt into the booth, you could build a two-door air lock, with the space in between kept scrupulously clean.

When the spray booth is in use, the floors need to be dampened with water. Some woodworkers cover the walls of the booth with white liner paper pinned to the walls so that the spray drift can be seen. Generally speaking, if your spray-painting environment is controlled and you are safe, it follows that your procedures are likely to be more effective and the results successful.

See also: workshop / solution 1 / page 12

---

solution 4

DENIBBING

If you wet a piece of wood, or seal it with a thin coat of varnish or shellac and let it dry, the grain will feather up to some extent, so that it feels hairy to the touch. Before you can achieve a super-smooth surface, these feathers or grain hairs need to be sanded off. The hairs are called "nibs," and the procedure of sanding them off is called "denibbing." In denibbing, you dampen the surface with water after the final sanding, let it dry, and then sand the nibs off with the finest grade of paper.

See also: sanding / solution 1 / page 102

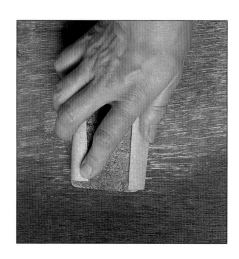

LEFT Use a block and the finest grade of abrasive paper to cut back the nibs of raised grain.

40 My varnished surface has not dried smooth. What is the problem? How can I make it look good? How can I achieve a foolproof finish?

ABOVE A rough varnished surface looks bad and feels worse!

STRIPPING

If your varnished surface is an irreversible mess, then the first step is to strip it to the bare wood. This is certainly an unpleasant, backbreaking task, but it is the only way to create the surface you want. While I always choose to use a cabinet scraper whenever possible—I much prefer to scrape dry—there are times when the best bet is to use a chemical stripper. The first thing to say here is that chemical strippers are potentially very dangerous—nasty for the eyes, lungs and skin. You must wear goggles, gloves and old throwaway clothes. You must work in a well-ventilated area—better outdoors—and you must always follow the manufacturer's instructions to the letter. I usually wear a full ventilator mask and an easy-to-wash cotton hat. I also know of woodworkers who wear barrier creams on their faces—especially on their eyelids and lips. And of course, once the stripping is finished, you must neutralize the surface, and you must dispose of the mess in the way advised by your local health and safety department. Not only all this, but some chemical strippers are also flammable! Note—don't forget to wear old shoes—it's a real drag when you get a blob of stripper on a nice pair of dress shoes!

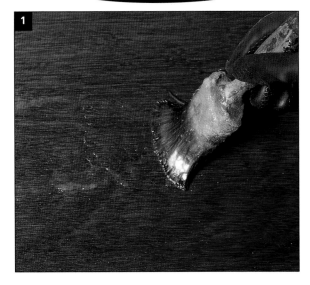

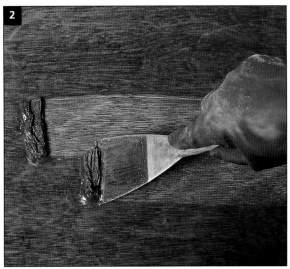

1 When you have carefully selected a type of chemical stripper to suit your particular piece of woodwork—that is, its age, value, form, the type of wood, and the type of finish—and when you have a clear idea of what to do if you get the stripper on your skin or in your eyes, and when you have donned various suitable old clothes, goggles and gloves, and when you have put the pets and children out of harm's way, then you are ready to get started. Begin by laying the stripper on in great gobs—so that it is layered thickly on the surface.

2 Allow the fully recommended time for the stripping solution to soak into the old finish. Don't be impatient and try scraping it off too soon—that would be just a waste of time and energy. You can try a trial scrape every few minutes or so, to see if it has loosened enough. When the surface starts to bubble and heave, scrape the whole mess off and

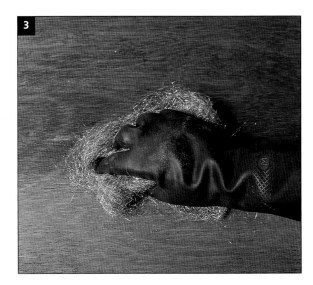

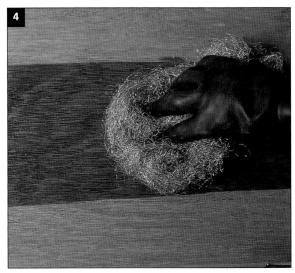

wipe it onto sheets of newspaper. Work in the direction of the grain, with the scraper held at a low angle. Don't force the pace and risk scratching the wood or leaving any undissolved finish behind.

3 After cleaning off as much finish as possible with the scraper, give the surface another thin coat of stripper, and then scrub the whole surface with a pad of steel wool of a grade to suit your wood. Work in the direction of the grain.

4 Finally, when you have removed all traces of the old finish, neutralize the surface with the recommended agent—mineral spirits, warm water, a soda water solution, or whatever is recommended on the label.

See also scraper / solution 5 / page 43

solution 2

OILING

If you are looking for a quick, easy-to-do finish to replace the varnish, then perhaps oil is the answer. Certainly it's not as durable as some finishes, and it takes longer to dry, but it's wonderfully easy to apply. There are nowadays many choices of oil, but linseed oil takes some beating. While oils tend to be pretty user-friendly, you do have to be very careful with oil-soaked rags and steel wool—they can self-combust. You should dispose of them in a proper way—burning the rags out of doors, for instance.

1 Clean and scrape your surface to a smooth-to-the-touch finish.

2 Brush the oil liberally over the whole surface. Wipe off the excess.

3 Allow the oil to dry overnight—longer with some oils—and then take a soft lint-free cloth and burnish the surface to a high-sheen finish.

See also: sanding / solution 2 / page 95

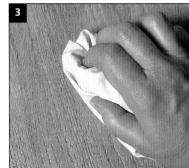

WIRE BRUSHING

Wire brushing has got to be one of the lowest of low-tech solutions! All you do is take a common or garden-variety wire brush—the type that you use for cleaning rusty iron pots, for instance—and brush your chosen wood in the direction of the grain. While this might sound a bit primitive, it is possible to create the most beautiful weathered-looking surfaces—resembling pieces of driftwood that have been washed and weathered by the sea, or the pieces of wood that you see in the desert. The technique works best with woods that have big, bold grain patterns, like oak and pine.

To my way of thinking, this technique looks best when it is used to create a contrast with a surface that is smooth and sophisticated. For example, I built a set of armchairs in the early twentieth century European tradition, made from American oak and with fancy brass fittings. I was so disappointed with the rather bland, planed finish that I decided I had nothing to lose by giving them the wire-brush treatment. Well, I have got to tell you, they now look wonderful! The contrast between the scoured out grain and the smooth brass fittings is perfect.

See also: grain / solution 1 / page 94

ABOVE Use a steel wire brush to cut out the soft grain. Always work in the direction of the grain.

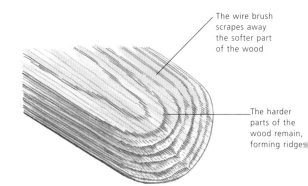

The wire brush scrapes away the softer part of the wood

The harder parts of the wood remain, forming ridges

ABOVE A rough wire-brushed finish imitating wood worn away by weather can look beautiful.

LEFT This plain little box has been vigorously wire-brushed so that the end grain surfaces look as if they have been worn and weathered.

BEESWAX

Of all the finishes, beeswax is—all at the same time—
one of the cheapest, one of the easiest to apply, one of
the oldest, and one of the most beautiful. Though
there is considerable disagreement on the best recipe,
with some woodworkers preferring a mix of beeswax
and various other waxes, I suggest a simple mix of 1 lb
of pure beeswax with 3/4 pint of pure turpentine. All I
do is push the wax through a cheese grater, put the
resulting flakes in a double saucepan, and pour in
enough turps to cover. I then warm up the mix like oat-
meal. When the wax has dissolved, I add a little more
turps until the mix is sloppy—like very soft butter.

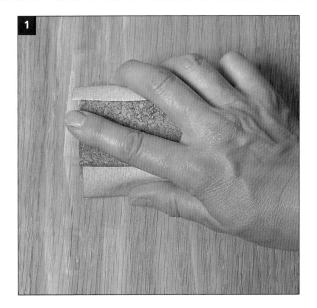

Of course a waxed finish isn't as hard as other finishes, but to my way of thinking this is more than offset by
the fact that a beeswax finish can be reworked by applying more wax and re-burnishing. As to the criticism
made by some woodworkers that a beeswaxed finish
tends to darken as it is handled, I think that it is just a
mix of ingrained dust and skin oil from hands—and that
it gives the wax a unique patina and depth of color. And
as for the complaint that a beeswaxed finish feels slightly sticky to the touch, to my mind it is the slight tackiness
under the fingertips plus the beautiful smell that gives a
beeswax finish its appealing character.

1 Wipe the surface with a mineral spirit-dampened
cloth, and then rub the surface down with a block
wrapped with self-lubricating silicon-carbide abrasive
sandpaper. Work in the direction of the grain until the
surface feels smooth to the touch. Every now and then
wipe the surface with the spirit, and look at the high-
lighted surface to see if the grain is hairy (nibbed).

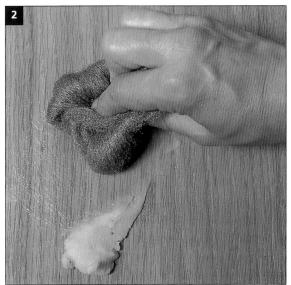

2 Swab the surface with a generous amount of
beeswax and use a pad of fine steel wool to work the
wax into the grain. Repeat this procedure five or six
times until you are happy with the finish. Some woodworkers advocate leaving the wax to harden between
applications.

3 Finally, take a pad of lint-free cotton cloth and burnish the surface to a sheen. Rub with a light, quick
stroke. An often asked question is, do subsequent wax-
ings improve upon the one before? Some woodworkers
consider that building up depth of shine in this way is
all baloney and old wives' tales—I can only say that I
think that the more coats the merrier.

See also: wax filler / solution 3 / page 73

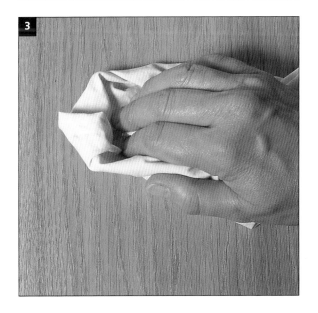

41 In an effort to speed up some staining, I mixed a water-based dye with a solvent to make the dye light-fast and not raise the grain. Sadly the mix dried to an ugly color. How can I redo it?

ABOVE An unstable, badly colored finish not only looks ugly, but worse yet, it might react unpredictably with later finishes and polishes.

solution 1

BLEACHING

One solution is to lighten the color with bleach. Depending on the density and chemistry of the finish, the bleach should tone down the color. Because the color might look worse, it would be best to test the bleach on a small corner first and see what it does. Just brush the bleach on, wait for the recommended time, wipe it off and brush on the neutralizer. As with chemical stripper, when working with bleach you must wear goggles and protective clothes (including rubber gloves and apron) and work in a well-ventilated area.

See also: labeling / solution 7 / page 13

LEFT After waiting for the bleach to react, wipe it off with a pad of clean cloth.

solution 2

ADDING A COLOR WASH

If you can't (or don't want to) bleach the color, then you can camouflage it with a diluted spirit dye or stain. All you do is mix the dye or stain with a methanol-based thinner until you have a thin translucent color, and then wipe it on. The idea is to modify the underlying color little by little with each coat until you are happy with the result.

1 Mix your chosen spirit dye or stain—anything from a light orange to a rich red brown—with the thinner. Try it out on a small edge of the piece. Wait until it is dry; you can't see the true effect until then. When you have the mix you want, apply it with a wide, soft brush, and make sure that the brush marks are going in the direction of the grain.

2 If after you have applied the first coat you aren't happy with the effect, then repeat the procedure until it is what you want. Remember that the color will darken after each coat. If the brushed coat is too uniform, you can break it up by variously dabbing and stroking with a cloth.

See also: paint effects / solutions 1–4 / pages 102–3

solution 3

VARNISH GLAZE

If you are a bit of an artist, then you will enjoy experimenting with varnish glazes. You need a tin of clear, high-gloss spar varnish and a selection of artist's oil colors. Be wary here—you don't want thixotropic gel varnish, and you don't want artist's acrylic paint. Go for the brown-yellow-red range of oil colours if you want to imitate mahogany. However, there is no reason not to cover the existing finish with a color that bears no relationship to wood colors.

1 Add a small worm of oil color to the varnish, stir it together and apply the resulting mix as a glaze. Do not add too much oil color, do not mix in all the varnish at once, and try it out a number of times before you apply the glaze to the piece. Use a good-quality brush and lay the varnish on with soft even strokes— first diagonally and then with the grain.

2 Wait for the varnish to harden, and then soften the surface by rubbing it down with fine-grade steel wool. Work in the direction of the grain with a light, even pressure. Finally, work a little beeswax into the surface and burnish it to a sheen.

See also: clear filler / solution 2 / page 72

       brushwork solution / solution 3 / page 103

       paint effect / solution 4 / page 103

solution 4

USING WATER-BASED DYE

Water-based stains are a good deal less expensive than spirit-based stains, but they are more unpredictable and difficult to apply. But if you take care with the preparation, a water stain is a very effective way of coloring wood.

1 Scrape the surface down to bare wood and clean off all traces of the previous finish. It's vital that the surface be completely free from grease, old paint, varnish and glue. Brush the wood clean and sweep up the debris. Move the workpiece to a clean, dust-free area that you have set aside for finishing.

2 Choose your powder color and mix it with water, following the directions. Try it out on a scrap of wood and let it dry. When you have what you consider is a good color, swab the wood down with clean water and brush on the stain. Keep the color moving, making sure that the edge of the stained area doesn't dry.

3 Use a clean, dry cloth to wipe off the stain in the direction of the grain. Finally, when the surface is dry, use a fine grade of abrasive to smooth off the nibs for a perfect finish.

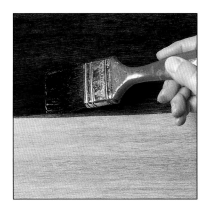

ABOVE Use a wide, soft brush to wipe on the water dye in the direction of the grain.

ABOVE Use a clean cloth to wipe off in the direction of the grain.

42 I gave my folk art chest a coat of green paint, but I find that the effect is too glossy and overpowering. How can I improve its looks?

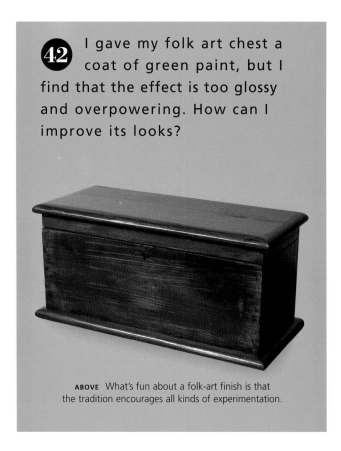

ABOVE What's fun about a folk-art finish is that the tradition encourages all kinds of experimentation.

solution 1

DISTRESSING AND WAXING

If you are looking for an easy solution, then this is it. All you need is sandpaper, wood wax and plenty of elbow grease.

1 Wrap your sandpaper around a block and sand the whole chest down, with the grain. Concentrate on exposed edges and corners.

2 Wax the surface and burnish to a high shine.

See also: sanding / solution 4 / page 95

color wash / solution 2 / page 100

solution 2

DABBED COLORS

If you are not keen on sanding away a glossy finish, then you can dab other colors over it with crumpled newspaper.

1 Select three colors that complement the chest and its setting. To subdue a glossy green, I would choose light green, pink and brick red. You can use oil paint or quick-drying acrylic. Do not thin the paint. Smear the colors on pieces of scrap wood, to create three separate palettes.

2 Crumple a piece of newspaper, and begin dabbing. Dab the newspaper into the color and press it onto the piece—dab and press, dab and press, and so on. Work through the colors, continually adjusting the balance to suit.

3 When the work is dry, use a pad of steel wool and distress the new finish as described above. Lastly, burnish with the wax polish.

See also: bleach / solution 1 / page 100

solution 3

STIPPLING

Stippling is another easy fix. The fact that the piece is already painted and too glossy is all to the good. Simply load a brush with paint and then dab and twist the brush on the surface you wish to decorate. To determine the final pattern you want, try out the technique on a sheet of newspaper first.

1 Select a stippling color darker than the paint on the chest. For a sharp stippling effect, use a stiff brush. For one that is slightly blurred, use a brush that is soft and full. I used a soft brush. Load the brush with paint, dab the excess off on a sheet of newspaper, and randomly dab the piece.

2 When the paint has dried slightly, use a clean brush to rework the stippled surface to suit. You might drag the brush to create a grain effect, or twist it, or otherwise use it to create a pattern to your liking.

See also: brushwork / solution 3 / page 101

solution 4

BULL'S EYE MARBLING

If you like swirling patterns, this may be a solution. The strong overall effect is similar to malachite marble, from which it draws its inspiration. You need three paint colors—pale green matte acrylic, medium green oil glaze and blue-black green oil glaze.

1 Give the chest an overall coat of the pale green acrylic, let it dry, and then brush on the medium green glaze. Create many vigorous brush marks as you work.

2 Use the same brush and apply a bit more pressure to create a tracked, overlapping effect.

3 While the medium green is still wet, overbrush the dark green glaze in much the same way, but this time leave areas open to show the underlying texture of the medium green.

4 Lastly, take the brush between your thumb and index finger and go over the whole surface, twisting to create the bull's eyes.

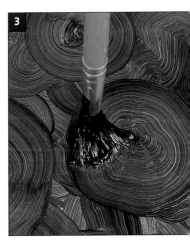

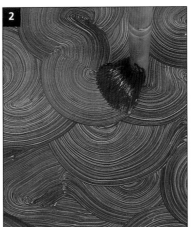

Handtool Care

Keeping up your handtools is one of the greatest pleasures of woodworking. One moment you have a plane, chisel or gouge that chews and splinters, and the next moment—after a bit of honing, adjustment and burnishing—you have a sharp, cleanly working tool that is a joy to use.

43 My children have been using my chisels and the edges are chipped and dull. How can I resharpen them and put them in good order? (The tools, that is!)

GRINDING TO REMOVE CHIPS

If the cutting edge of a chisel is nicked, the edge will need to be squared. If the nicks are small, they can usually be touched up with a file or on a coarse benchstone, but if they are deep, the edge will need regrinding on a wheel. Wheel grinding is done in three steps—squaring off to take out the nicks, polishing the back, and grinding the primary bevel. To square off the leading edge, set the rest so that it is horizontal (180°) to the surface of the wheel. Lay the chisel on the rest with the bevel uppermost, and grind the chisel on the wheel, moving it from side to side until you have ground back the leading edge to the depth of the deepest nick. When done, lay the blade flat on a benchstone, again with the bevel uppermost, and make a few circular strokes to polish the back of the blade. Finally, adjust the tool rest

LEFT A combination stone of Hard Arkansas and Washita.

LEFT A man-made stone—the fast-cutting 'Crystolon'.

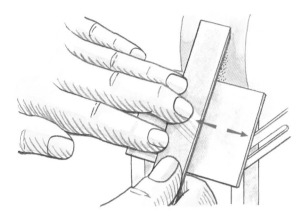

ABOVE Lay the chisel bevel side down on the stone and rub it from side to side. Be careful not to overheat the steel.

to an angle of about 25° to the wheel, lay the chisel with the bevel flat against the wheel, and grind it against the wheel, moving from side to side, just enough to establish the bevel angle. When using a bench grinder, don't grind off too much metal, and don't allow the blade to overheat—and always wear goggles!

See also: diamond stone / solution 3 / page 106

plane iron honing / solution 5 / page 109

ABOVE Though the bench grinder enables you to swiftly grind back to a true edge, you do have to repeatedly dip the blade in water to keep down the temperature.

LEFT Hold the guide firm and square so that the movement is even and controlled.

HONING WITH A GAUGE

Once grinding on the wheel is done, hone the bevel on a benchstone to polish it. If you are a novice, use a honing guide or gauge. Position the chisel in the guide bevel down, and set the angle to place the bevel flat against the stone. Dribble a few drops of light oil on the stone, and then hone the chisel backwards and forwards. With experience, you can dispense with the guide—many woodworkers say it develops better hand-eye coordination without.

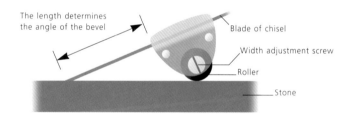

The length determines the angle of the bevel

Blade of chisel

Width adjustment screw

Roller

Stone

ABOVE Side view of a sharpening guide. The guide is helpful in that it maintains a square edge. It is crucial that you follow the instructions that come with it–they will tell you how far the blade should protrude for the different bevels.

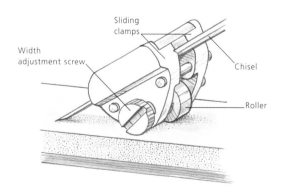

Sliding clamps

Width adjustment screw

Chisel

Roller

ABOVE Lay the chisel bevel side down in the gauge, tighten up the adjustment screw slightly so that the blade is captured, make fine adjustments until you have the correct bevel-to-stone angle, and then tighten the screw.

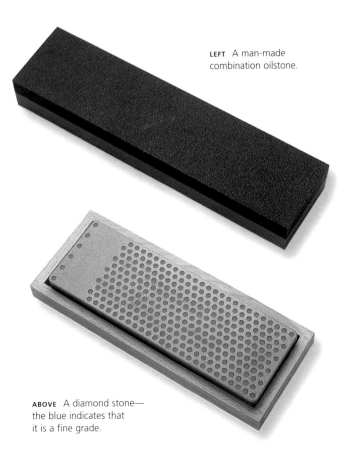

LEFT A man-made combination oilstone.

ABOVE A diamond stone—the blue indicates that it is a fine grade.

HONING ON A DIAMONDSTONE

Many woodworkers advocate using a diamond-stone. The manufacturers claim that such stones will cut up to 95% faster than conventional oil and water stones. Diamondstones are graded from extra coarse to extra fine, and can be used for everything from grinding to fine honing.

1 Many woodworkers feel that polishing the back of a chisel blade—after the leading edge has been ground square, and before honing the primary bevel—is at the heart of successful chisel sharpening. The object is to flatten the back of the chisel so that all traces of the burr have been removed. A diamondstone is perfect for this because it is exceptionally flat.

2 Place the chisel flat on the stone, apply pressure with your fingertips, and work with a firm circular action. With precision and the right pressure, a few strokes are all that is needed.

3 After the primary bevel is ground comes the much maligned polishing of the secondary bevel. I say maligned, because this stage has been variously described as a waste of time, difficult to achieve and fussy. What you do is sprinkle a few drops of water

HONING A GOUGE

Honing a gouge is more or less identical to honing a chisel, but more difficult because the gouge blade is curved. Many woodworkers advocate honing with the stone on the bench. I prefer to hold the stone up, at eye level. By seeing close up the light shining between the stone and the bevel, I am better able to maintain the bevel angle around the curve. A good test of sharpness after honing is to cut the end grain of a piece of hardwood like maple. If you got it right, chisels and gouges should slice smoothly.

1 With the stone held in one hand and the gouge in the other—touch the bevel to the stone and appraise the angle of the bevel looking at the amount of light shining between the two surfaces. This done, hold the stone perfectly still, while at the same time rocking the gouge so that the full curve of the bevel comes into contact.

2 When you have achieved the primary and sec-ondary bevels, take a small shaped slip, hold it at a

comfortable angle, and run it a couple of times over the inside-curve-edge—so as to remove the minute burr.

3 Finally, take a fold of stiff leather and strop both the outside bevel and the inside-curve, by burnish-ing the surface to a high shine finish. And just in case you think that stropping is a load of hooey—some woodworkers do—then I suggest that you test the edge before and after stropping!

See also: grinding / solution 1 / page 104

on the stone, set the chisel bevel face down so that the whole bevel is in full contact with the stone, and then raise the handle slightly so that a bead of water pushes out in front of the blade. Then draw the chisel towards you with a careful dragging action. If you then hold the bevel up to a light, you will see that a secondary bevel or microbevel can be seen as a thin line of light running along the cutting edge.

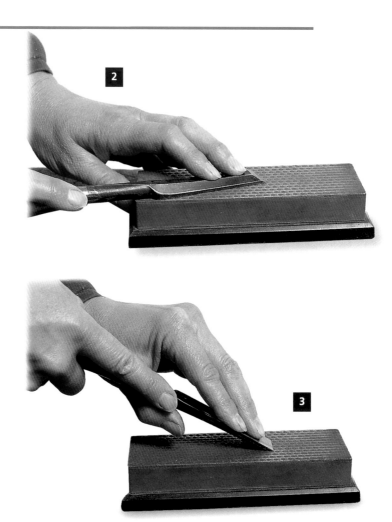

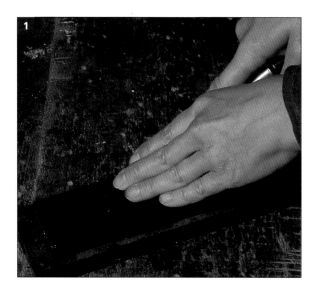

44 My smooth plane has left a pattern of tiny furrows on a tabletop. What is the problem? How can I adjust the plane so that it does not make furrows?

RIGHT A hand plane is a wonderful tool, but only if it's clean, sharp and properly adjusted.

solution 1

STRIPPING DOWN

Your plane is out of adjustment. The bench plane, a tool at the very heart of woodwork, is yet one of the most abused tools in the workshop. The success of the cutting action depends not only on the iron being sharp, but also on all the parts being properly adjusted. The challenge is to achieve a balance of all the adjustments.

First strip the plane down to its component parts.
1 Lift the cam and pull up and remove the lever cap. Draw the plane iron cap and plane iron up towards the handle and ease it forward and up, so that it clears the lever cap screw.
2 Undo the cap iron screw, and separate the cap and plane iron by turning the cap around and down—so that it is at right angles to the iron—and then slide it down towards the cutting edge until the screw head is clear of the slot.
3 Undo and remove the screw at the back of the frog and the two screws at the front of the frog, and lift the frog clear.
4 Turn the adjusting nut clockwise so that it clears the Y-shaped adjusting lever.
5 Finally, unscrew the single screw that attaches the front knob to the toe and the two screws that attach the back handle to the heel.

See also: tuning a plane / solution 3 / page 41

solution 2

LAPPING THE IRON AND IRON CAP

Lapping is the procedure of flattening, removing rust, and polishing. It is done on a lapping board, which is a sheet of flat material—a board, a sheet of plate glass or whatever—on which is mounted a sheet of fine-grade abrasive paper with the abrasive side facing up. Something like silicon carbide, garnet or aluminum oxide works well. I usually mount the paper with double-sided sticky tape. If you choose to mount the paper on a sheet of glass, support it on a piece of board so the glass does not break.

1 Dribble a few drops of oil on the grit, lay the plane iron cap on it, top up, and lap the underside edge to a perfectly smooth finish. The idea is to flatten the underside edge, so that it meets the iron absolutely flush, leaving no room for shavings to push up between the two pieces.

2 Lap both sides of the plane iron until the metal is free from high spots and polished smooth. The iron must be pressed flat throughout the whole operation.

See also: lapping / solution 1 / page 111

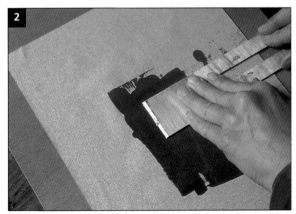

solution 3

LAPPING THE SOLE

Just like the plane iron, the body of the plane should be lapped to flatten the sole (bottom). The frog, knob and handle should be attached to the body.

1 Use a pad of fine grade steel wool and mineral spirits to clean off all traces of rust and resin. Color the sole and the sides of the plane with a felt tip marker.

2 Dribble a few drops of light oil on the lapping board grit, and begin stroking the sole of the plane backward and forward. Continue until the whole sole is bright and gleaming. Repeat for the sides.

See also: lapping / solution 1 / page 111

solution 4

CLEARING THE FROG

As part of getting your plane in good order, the frog must also be cleaned, oiled and correctly adjusted.

Start by brushing the dust and debris out of the various nooks and crannies. Pay particular attention to the area behind the lateral adjusting lever. Lightly oil it and the Y-shaped adjusting lever so that both move freely. Set the frog back in place so that it is very slightly back from the mouth, and then tighten up the three screws.

Reinstall the adjusting nut, making sure it fits into the Y lever. Make sure that the leading edge of the frog is square with the mouth.

See also: smoothing plane /solution 4 / page 43

ABOVE RIGHT If the lateral adjusting lever is stiff, chances are there is a mix of wood dust and oil packed between the lever and the body of the frog. Clean it out with a small brush.

solution 5

HONING THE PLANE IRON

Just like a chisel, the plane iron has two bevels—a primary bevel and a secondary microbevel. The honing procedure is much the same as for the chisel.

1 First hone the primary bevel to an angle of about 25°, and then cock the iron up at an angle that is slightly greater than the primary bevel and hone the microbevel. Use a honing guide if you want to take the guesswork out of setting the angles.

2 Reassemble the plane, and adjust the nut for depth of cut. Push the lateral adjusting lever left or right to set the cutting edge of the iron parallel with the plane mouth.

See also: diamond stone / solution 3 / page 106

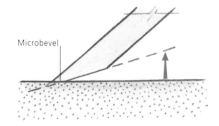

Microbevel

ABOVE The microbevel is honed by laying the primary bevel flat on the stone, lifting the blade slightly, and fine honing just the front edge of the bevel.

45 I have been given a set of beautiful old handsaws, unfortunately all dull. What is the best way to sharpen them?

CLEANING

Make sure the blade and handle are sound. The handle must be free from splits, and the blade must be reasonably flat along its length, and free from deeply pitted areas, kinks and fractures. Undo the nuts, remove the handle, and rub the blade down with a pad of steel wool and mineral spirits or polish. Then replace the handle and tighten the nuts. Burnish the blade and polish the handle and nuts for appearance, and wipe the blade with light machine oil or lemon-oil furniture polish after each use.

See also: beeswax / solution 4 / page 99

See also: beeswax / solution 4 / page 99

solution 1

LEFT Go easy when you remove the nuts—make sure your screwdriver is a good fit.

LEFT Be careful not to damage the brass medallion; it is usually a guide to the quality and value of old saws.

solution 2

SHARPENING

Sharpening is done in three stages: jointing, or filing the teeth tips to the same level; setting, or bending the teeth out alternately to one side or the other to widen the kerf; and fitting or filing, cutting the gullet angle with a file in order to sharpen the teeth for cutting.

■ Fit a crosscut saw by filing the teeth at an angle of 65° to the blade. Use a small three-cornered file, and cut the bevel on both teeth, working through every other gullet. Then reverse the blade and repeat through the alternate gullets.

■ Fit ripsaw teeth by filing them at right angles (90°) to the saw blade. Cut alternate teeth, and repeat from the other side. Secure the blade low in the vise so it does not judder as you cut.

■ In setting, you use a special tool called a saw set. Clamp the saw blade in a vise. Adjust the saw set to the correct number of points per inch, based on the manufacturer's directions. Position the tool on each tooth leaning away, and bend the top half of the tooth. Do this on every other tooth on one side of the blade, and then reverse to do the ones in between.

ABOVE For a rip saw, the file is held at right angles to the blade and ground straight across.

ABOVE Adjust the saw set dial to suit the saw size, position it in place on the next tooth in the sequence, and gently squeeze the handles together.

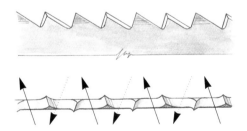

ABOVE Note how with the same stroke filing creates two bevels on opposite sides of neighboring teeth.

46 I have an old oilstone, but it is clogged, glazed and uneven. Can it be renewed? What is the best way to house it?

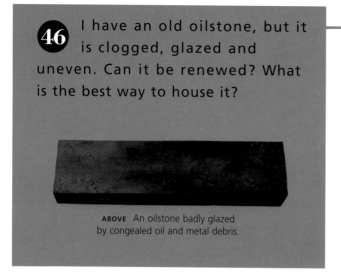

ABOVE An oilstone badly glazed by congealed oil and metal debris.

---

solution 1

CLEANING AND LAPPING

Clean oilstones with mineral spirits. Flood the surface and let it soak so that all the ground-in muck and grunge will wipe away. If the surface is sticky with blobs of resin, use a stiff brush to clean them off. Be sure to wear goggles and rubber gloves. After cleaning, and to flatten the surface, color the face of the stone with a black felt tip marker pen, and then rub the stone face on a lapping board until the color has worn away. Some woodworkers recommend using a diamond-stone to lap old oilstones.

See also: lapping / solutions 2–3 /
pages 108–9
honing / solution 5 /
page 109

LEFT Rub the stone across the abrasive paper on the lapping board to level the face of the stone.

ABOVE RIGHT Flood the surface of the stone with spirit to remove the muck.

---

solution 2

TRADITIONAL AND STEPPED TRAYS

The traditional solution to holding and protecting your stone is to build a recessed wooden tray, with wooden ends to prevent the stone from getting rounded over, a lid to cover the stone, and the underside fitted with spikes like a golf shoe that drive into the bench top to hold it steady. Beyond that, many woodworkers advocate attaching the tray to a stepped base so it can be secured in a vise. This makes sure the tray stays put when you are honing. To do this, ease the stone from the tray, and run three or four countersunk brass screws through the base of the tray into a piece of 1 in. hardwood narrower than the tray. Return the stone. The step is gripped in the vise, and the downward pressure goes on the jaws of the vise.

See also: workshop / solution 2 / page 12

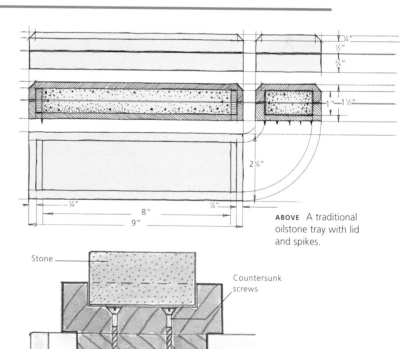

ABOVE A traditional oilstone tray with lid and spikes.

Stone

Countersunk screws

Bench

Hardwood block

LEFT A stepped oilstone tray design for clamping in a vise.

Keeping up Power Tools

Power tools are great, but only when they are working well. If you have a tool that is below par, and you want to make it work better, or you want to know how to make jigs that will enable you to reach new levels of performance with your power tools, then the following solutions could be the answer.

47 My band saw blade is broken again! The saw is not correctly set or I am using the wrong blade. How should I properly adjust it?

---

solution 1

CHOOSING THE BEST BLADE FOR THE JOB

Apart from the pitch of the blade—the size and number of teeth to the inch—the main factor that influences the way a band saw blade cuts and how long it lasts is its width. The basic rule of thumb is that the wider the blade the straighter the cut, and the narrower blade the tighter the cut. Ask yourself these questions: What do you need to cut small, tight curves? What do you need to cut straight lines? I tend to use three blade sizes: a ³⁄₁₆ in. blade for cutting curves down to a radius of ½ in., a ¼ in. blade for curves down to a radius of ¾ in., and a ½ in. blade for general straight work. If you try to cut a small curve with a wide blade or a thick section with a thin blade, then the blades are going to break!

See also: using power tools / solution 5 / page 13

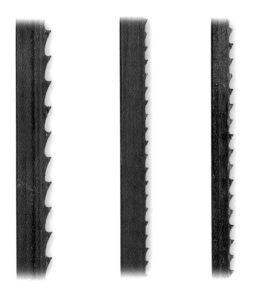

ABOVE You need a selection of blades of different widths and different teeth settings so that you can choose the best blade for the job.

solution 2

SANDING THE WHEELS

If the rubber tires around the wheels are worn at one edge, they can cause the blade to slide off track. If this is the case, then you need to sand the tires level. Start by pulling the plug and removing the blade. Wrap some sandpaper around a block, and hold the block against the tire while turning the wheel by hand. Do this with both wheels. If the tires are worn down to the rims, replace them.

See also: bearings / solution 5 / page 114

solution 3

INSTALLING A NEW BLADE

Unplug the saw. Set the worktable level and remove the pin or bolt from the front end of the table slot. Lift out the throat plate and put it to one side. Open the top and bottom covers to expose the wheels and blade. Remove the blade guard, or slide it well out of the way.

Put on your safety glasses and a pair of protective leather gloves. Ease off the tension so that the top wheel slides down and the blade slackens off. Now, very carefully, grip the blade with both hands and draw it forward so that it slips off the wheels. Slide the blade along the table slot and ease it out from between the guides.

When you have cleared the old blade from the machine, break it into short pieces by folding it up, and put it in the garbage bin. Grasp the new blade in both hands—making sure that it is well clear of your face. Ease the loops slightly apart and cast the blade on the floor so that it opens up. Wipe any excess grease off the blade. Arrange the blade so that the teeth face down toward the worktable.

Slide the blade through the table slot, ease it between the guides, and set it in place on the wheels. Finally, at one and the same time, adjust the top wheel to tension the blade and turn the wheel over by hand so that the blade stays on track.

solution 4

ADJUSTING BLADE TRACKING

1 Making sure that the blade tracks properly also involves adjusting the tilt mechanism of the top wheel. However, you may wish to begin by verifying that both wheels are aligned and parallel with each other. First put a straightedge across both wheels to assess how much they are out of alignment, and then move one or other wheel out along its shaft by using washers to shim it. To do this, you must remove the wheel, slide the washers on the shaft and then replace the wheel.

2 Once the wheels are in line with one another, revolve them by hand in order to make sure that the blade stays centered on the top wheel. If it slides off, adjust the tilt mechanism and repeat until the blade stays (tracks) in the center. Then tighten everything up, replace the covers and guards, and run the saw to verify that the blade is tracking as it should.

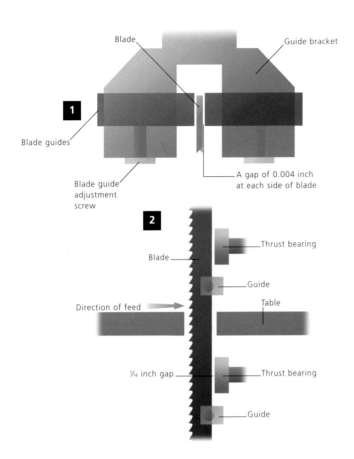

1

Blade

Guide bracket

Blade guides

Blade guide adjustment screw

A gap of 0.004 inch at each side of blade

2

Blade

Thrust bearing

Guide

Direction of feed

Table

¹⁄₁₆ inch gap

Thrust bearing

Guide

SETTING THE GUIDES

If you look closely at the mechanism above the table, you will note that there is a blade support wheel that stops the blade being pushed too far back, and two guides, one on each side of the blade, that stop sideways and twisting movement. This whole mechanism is duplicated underneath the table. On most machines, this mechanism is attached to the blade guard or a guidepost. Pull the plug before making the following adjustments.

1 Adjust the guide blocks so that they pinch the blade, and then ease them back a tad. One manufacturer recommends a space of .004 in. at each side of the blade. Do this with all four guides.

2 Rotate the large wheels so that the blade weld is level with the small blade support wheel, and bring the support wheel up so that it just touches the back of the blade. Then ease the support wheel back until there is a space of about 1/16 in. between it and the weld. Rotate the blade again to check that the space is constant, and then lock the nuts. Do this with both support wheels.

See also: new blade / solution 3 / page 113

SETTING THE TABLE
AND PROVING THE CUT

If you are constantly struggling to hold the work-piece on course—and in so doing bending and twisting the blade—it may be that the table is set incorrectly. Start by pulling the plug and loosening the bolt or lever that locks the table. Then take a metal square, place it on the table so that one edge is against the side of the blade, and ease the table into square alignment and lock it. Rotate the blade a full revolution to check that it stays square with

the table. If the angle reading on your saw is incorrectly set, adjust it for a correct reading, or ignore it. To test or prove the cut, first take a planed board about 1 in. thick and 6 in. wide, and mark a line across it, top and bottom, with a square. Then switch on the band saw and cut in from one edge, stopping just short of half way across the board, flip the board over and cut in from the other edge. If the cuts meet head on, the table is correctly set. If they are slightly misaligned, you need to start over.

ABOVE Square the wood and mark center lines on both sides.

ABOVE Run the saw cut to stop just short of the center line.

ABOVE Flip the wood over and rerun a second cut towards the center line.

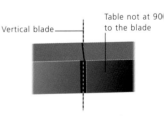

Vertical blade

Table not at 90 to the blade

ABOVE If—as shown, the table is out of true, then the second cut will be at an opposing angle to the first.

FINE TUNING

Fine tuning is defined as all the small maintenance procedures that go to keeping a tool working well. It might not seem too important if the worktable has some resin on it, or the casings are dusty, but if you add all these little nuisances together, you have a machine working below par. First check that the on/off switch is clean and fully functioning. Then pull the plug. Inspect the blade to make sure that it is free from kinks and wipe it with light machine oil. Oil the bearings. Vacuum all the dust out of the wheel casings. Wipe the worktable with a spirit-dampened cloth to remove resin and then polish it. Continue cleaning and oiling until the machine is finely tuned and sweetly running.

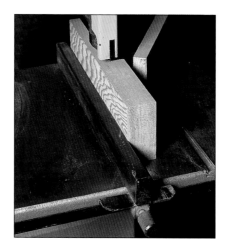

LEFT Use use the fence for support when you are resawing a board.

RESAWING

Resawing is defined as cutting a board in half through the edge. For example, if you have a 1 in. board and you saw it apart to make two ½ in. boards, then it has been resawn. It's not too difficult if the board is thick enough to stand on edge, but for anything thinner than 1 in., you need to use a fence. While in most instances the optional extra fence as supplied with most band saws is perfectly adequate, you may well need to build a higher fence for thin but wide boards. Always use the widest possible hook-tooth type band saw blade.

See also: finger jig / solution 9 / page 125

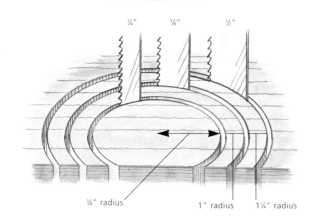

¼"   ⅜"   ½"

⅜" radius   1" radius   1¼" radius

CUTTING CURVES

If your band saw blades keep breaking, it could be that you are trying to cut curves with the wrong size blade and at the wrong speed. While you most certainly need smaller and smaller blade widths for smaller and smaller curves, you also need to match the speed at which you advance the wood to the thickness of the wood. For example, while a ¼ in. wide blade is a good choice for a radius of about ¾ in., the speed of cut will most certainly depend upon the thickness of the wood. The corollary rule of thumb is the thicker the wood, the slower the rate of feed.

See also: carving curves / solution 1 / page 88

sawing curves / solutions 1–2 / pages 24–5

ABOVE No matter how thick the wood, the rule is, the narrower the blade the tighter the curve.

TILTING TABLE

The tilt function on most band saw tables means that you can tilt the table to achieve a whole range of angled cuts from 90° to 45°. This is particularly good when you need to cut corner miters. While most band saws have an angle guide alongside the tilt mechanism, experience has taught me that this is usually inaccurate. The best bet is to set the angle with the guide and then double check with a bevel.

ABOVE RIGHT Never take the angle guide reading as correct; always double check with a sliding bevel or a protractor.

48 My router is not working well. I need it for a project I am working on now. Can I adjust it myself?

GENERAL EVERYDAY CLEANING

Routers soon get dirty! Wood dust gets in the air intake and in the springs, resin builds up on the base and the posts, and so on. A little dust and dirt can make a sensitive tool like a router stop working well. You should routinely clean out all the dust and debris, just as you might clean out the car after a trip. Start by vacuuming it well. Then spend time with a small brush getting the dust out of all the little nooks and crannies. Polish the poles and generally keep all the brightwork gleaming. After the cleaning, spray a small amount of very light oil on the various moving parts, and wipe the whole works with a lint-free cloth.

LEFT Clean away all the dust and resin and burnish the brightwork.

LEFT Spray a small amount of light oil over mating surfaces so the various parts are able to move freely.

REPLACING THE BRUSHES

If your router starts to spark and splutter, the brushes may need replacing. Start by pulling the plug and cleaning the work surface. You may have to unscrew a cap, or unscrew and remove part of the casing. The brushes are usually small carbon blocks held in place with springs. Hold the spring out of the way, ease the brush out of its channel and install a new brush.

RIGHT After pulling the plug and reading through the manual, ease the brushes out and check that they are free from cracks, are not too short, not clogged with debris, and so on.

Retaining spring

Brush channel

LONG-TERM CLEANING

Routers collect fine wood dust that works its way into all their component parts. So apart from the everyday cleaning described above, every now and again you need to strip down a router and give it a more thorough cleaning. Clean off the dust and wipe off resin buildup with spirits, and make sure all moving parts are clean and free-moving—but never be tempted to clean close-fitting parts with abrasives! Because router parts are designed to fine tolerances, abrasives would wreck them.

Instead, unscrew the various casings and housings, brush the dust out, check that all moving metal-to-metal parts travel easily, and wipe them with a thin film of light oil.

ABOVE RIGHT A buildup of fine wood dust and resin will eventually do harm; it should be removed before it causes problems.

solution 4

ABOVE A suspect chuck collet must be replaced immediately.

CHECKING THE CHUCK COLLETS

Router chucks must be painstakingly disassembled, inspected, and then reassembled at regular intervals. The reason is that you can't see if the collet splines are free from cracks just by looking. I once discovered a collet spline snapped off at its root. The only thing standing between me and catastrophe was lots of compacted dust! A damaged chuck collet is an accident waiting to happen. Always err on the side of safety and replace anything that looks suspect.

solution 5

VIBRATION PROBLEMS

If you are suddenly aware of an increase in router vibration, the best advice is to switch off the power, pull the plug, and give the whole tool a thorough inspection. Start by trying another bit. If this doesn't pinpoint the problem, tighten the chuck and try again, and so on. By looking at the various parts and trying out the router after each inspection, you should be able to identify the problem.

solution 6

PLUNGE ROUTER PROBLEMS

A common problem when using one of the large plunge routers is that the plunge function is intermittently stiff. And of course what inevitably happens is that you overcompensate, and the plunge either goes down in a series of jerks, or suddenly goes all the way down. The problem is usually caused by a buildup of resin on the posts, or by one or the other of the post springs being faulty, or by the knobs being stiff. Check out the posts and knobs, and wipe a small amount of light oil over the mating parts.

Check post springs

Build up of resin on posts

solution 7

NO POWER

If your router fails to start, unplug it, remove the bit, and start by looking at the plug. Check the order of wiring and the fuse. Next check the cable to make sure that it isn't broken inside. Finally, check the switch. If it is a sliding switch, make sure there isn't a buildup of fine dust behind it. Don't be tempted to break open any of the sealed units. Given the likelihood that you are more interested in woodwork than in electrical repair, there comes a time when the router needs to be sent away to be serviced. Of all the power tools, the router is perhaps the one that most needs to operate correctly. If you have any doubts about the way it is working, or the way you have cleaned it, then it is vital that you send it on its way to a recommended service center.

49 My table saw is not cutting squarely. How can I adjust and calibrate the table? What are the best procedures for using it?

solution 1

THE RIGHT BLADE FOR THE JOB

It is vital that you use the correct blade. The blades designed specifically for woodwork come in five basic types—the combination blade for general-purpose work, the crosscut blade for smooth cross-cutting, the rip blade for ripping down boards, the plywood blade designed to cut plywood properly, and the planer blade for fine joint work. While the combination blade is pretty good all around, it won't of course perform as well for a particular job as a dedicated blade.

See also: table saw / solution 1 / page 44

ABOVE LEFT Equip yourself with a good selection of different blades so that you can choose the best blade for the job.

solution 2

THROAT-PLATE DEBRIS

One problem to watch out for in using a table saw is accumulation of throat-plate debris. Wood dust is forced little by little under the throat plate, until the compacted dust lifts the edge and side of the plate slightly higher than the surrounding worktable, tipping the workpiece towards the blade. What starts out as a little bit of dust winds up as a cut out of square, and a throat plate raised just enough to stop the workpiece in its tracks! Simply remove the plate, clean out the dust, replace the plate—and then remember to brush the dust out after each use.

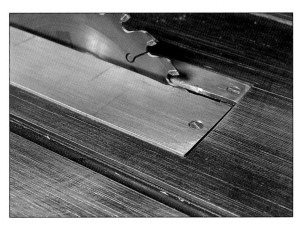

ABOVE The small sign of extra wear on the near side corner of the plate indicates that it is cocked slightly above the surrounding worktable.

solution 3

CHECKING SQUARENESS

A table saw must cut square, or it is useless. You therefore need to check squareness after changing blades and at regular intervals along the way.

1 Set an engineer's square in the miter slot so that it slides smoothly. Take two measurements, one from the front leading edge of the blade, and one from the back of the blade. If the two are identical, then the blade is aligned with the slot. If they are anything less than identical, you must realign the fence so that it is parallel to the edge of the miter slot.

2 Set the square up against the blade to check that the blade is at right angles to the table, and make adjustments accordingly.

3 Check the clearance between the blade and the throat plate.

solution 4

PROVING A SQUARE CUT

A cut less than true can spell disaster, so it's a good idea to prove squareness before use. The procedure is as follows.

1 Use a square to run a line across a piece of scrap board, aligned above and below. Butt the board up against the miter gauge and feed it into the blade. Run a cut half the width of the board.

2 Flip the board over and cut from the other edge. Stop short when the two cuts are about ⅛ in. apart.

3 If the two cuts meet, then squareness is proved. If they are out of alignment, you need to run checks on the blade, the table and the miter gauge.

See also: proving the cut / solution 6 / page 114

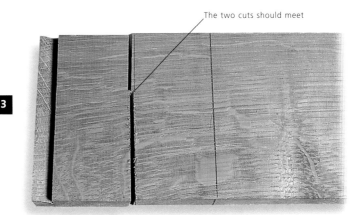

The two cuts should meet

solution 5

CLAMPING THE WORKPIECE

The best way to protect your fingers, and make your cuts with 100% accuracy, is to clamp the workpiece to the miter gauge. With the workpiece clamped to the gauge, you will be able to concentrate your efforts on controlling the rate of feed. In my rather primitive system, I use a C-clamp, but you can build a custom clamp by screwing a length of stock to the face of the miter gauge and mounting a toggle clamp to the stock piece.

See also: push-plane saw / solution 7 / page 124

ABOVE This setup enables you to crosscut accurately without fear of having your fingers too near the blade.

solution 6

TESTING SQUARENESS

Squaring the blade, the table, the miter gauge and the various fences are all aimed at the goal of making the cuts true. I usually start a project by running a trial cut with a piece of scrap wood and checking it with a top-grade engineer's square, and then adjusting the miter gauge accordingly. There is some debate on the accuracy of adjustable squares. Some

woodworkers insist on using the traditional fixed square.

LEFT Do a trial cut before every project, and check the accuracy with a square.

50 I made a hammer-and-nail jig, but it doesn't do the job. Can you give me a top-ten list of the most useful jigs? How are they made?

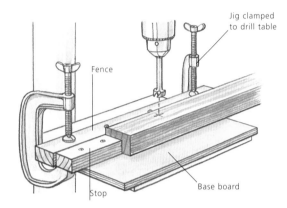

ABOVE A jig enables you to drill holes in the same place in a number of identical parts.

DRILL-PRESS JIG

One of the most useful jigs, and certainly one of the easiest to make, is the drill-press jig. It is simply a baseboard clamped to the drill-press worktable, with one or more pieces of wood screwed to the baseboard. In use, you first set up the jig to position the first hole or holes accurately, then bring the stops up to the sides of the workpiece. From then on you quickly and easily drill subsequent pieces without the need for measuring or brainpower.

Such a jig is a winner, in that the setup requires only the baseboard, a few pieces of scrap, and one or more clamps. If you want to go for something a little fancier, you can screw one or more toggle clamps to the baseboard, which locate the workpiece, and when the toggle clamps are clamped down you don't have to worry about holding the piece. This is a particularly good setup when you are using large-diameter Forstner drill bits.

See also: drill stop / solution 1 / page 62

forstner bits / solution 4 / page 11

drill press / solution 2 / page 71

DRILL-PRESS ANGLE JIG

Although you mostly drill holes at right angles to a workpiece, there are any number of situations in which you need to drill holes at some other angle. For example, you might want to drill angled holes into the underside of Windsor chair slabs so that the legs splay out, or stretcher holes in chair legs, or angled holes in toys, or whatever.

As with most jigs, the overall concept of the drill-press angle jig is almost too simple to be true. It is simply a pair of baseboards hinged together at one edge, like a book—so that it can be opened out and fixed at the desired angle. To hold the angle in a fixed position, you could use a cupboard stay at each side of the book, or a pair of through bolts with nuts that can be reset to change the angle, or whatever.

Otherwise, if you know that you are going to drill holes repeatedly at the same angle—say stretcher holes in turned chair legs—then it might be just as well to make a fixed jig dedicated to that purpose. In this case, you would need to make a long board that sits in a wedge-shaped block—with the wedge block cut to the desired angle, and the board with various stop slots and blocks to hold the workpiece.

See also: drilling jig / solution 6 / page 123

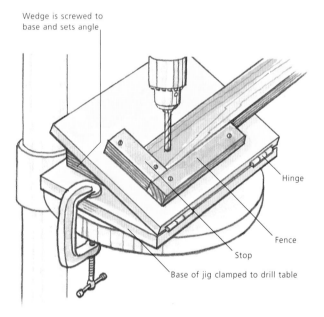

ABOVE The angle jig enables you to drill holes at a preset angle in a number of identical parts.

ROUTER TABLE

A bench-top router table is a versatile and easy-to-make jig that will enable you to perform a whole range of grooving and molding operations. It is simply a small table with a hinged top and a hole cut in the top, so that the router can be easily and quickly mounted with a minimum of fuss and effort. With the router in place, the top down, and an adjustable fence and a miter gauge groove in place, you can smoothly and precisely push wood past the bit.

This jig is easy to make, inexpensive, and it can be up and running in the space of a weekend. The table consists of a 1-in. sheet of best-quality plywood mounted on a box frame open on all four sides. For ease of construction and overall rigidity, I made the table from three frames joined with open mortise-and-tenon joints, and bolted the three frames together. However, there's no reason why you can't make the box sides from sheet ply, or use an old coffee table, or whatever.

The surface is hinged to the box shape with two or more solid hinges. To mount the router to the surface, all I did was cut a good-sized hole through the surface to take the base of my router, cut a lip in the top edge of the hole to a depth of ¼ in., and then drop a sheet of ¼ in. clear plastic in the hole so that it fitted flush like a window.

In use, the router is mounted to the plastic so that it hangs upside down, with the bit poking up through a central hole in the plastic. The slotted fence rides on two bolts, and the miter gauge runs in a groove.

See also: bolt-fitting / solution 2 / page 53

routers / pages 54–7

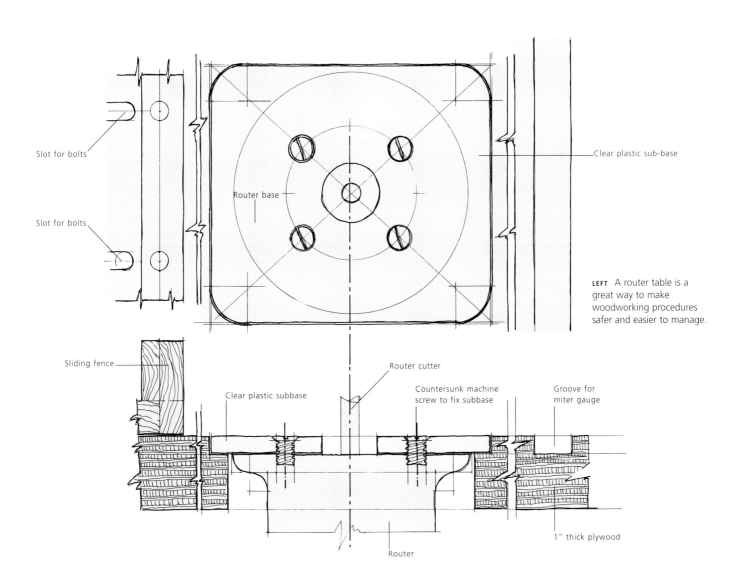

Slot for bolts

Slot for bolts

Router base

Clear plastic sub-base

LEFT A router table is a great way to make woodworking procedures safer and easier to manage.

Sliding fence

Clear plastic subbase

Router cutter

Countersunk machine screw to fix subbase

Groove for miter gauge

1" thick plywood

Router

SPINDLE-MOLDING JIG

This spindle jig is a clever item I designed specific-ally to enable me to run a molding along two edges of a slab of wood. I wanted to make a number of identical wallplates to go behind my electric switch-es, to match existing plates. Yes, I'm not sure wooden plates behind switches are a safe idea, but the concept could be modified for all manner of plates and bases. You can make bases for trophies, box lids, parts for toys, and so on. The idea is that the workpiece is secure, the result can be repeated, and your hands are safe.

1 Slide the workpiece into the recess.

2 Having first made sure that the workpiece is well aligned and flush with the jig, then turn the buttons so that it is safely contained.

3 Butt the jig hard up against the fence–so that the workpiece is to the right hand side of the cutter–switch on the power, and make a single pass from the right through to the left.

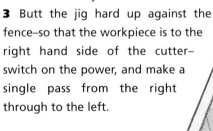

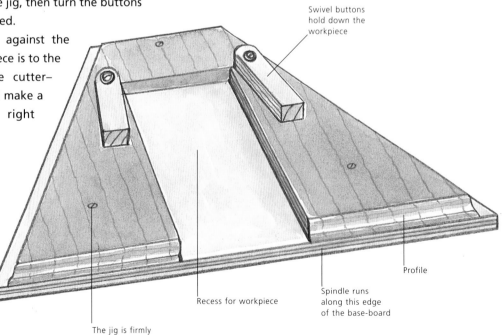

RIGHT This jig is the basis for all spindle molding jigs. The workpiece is held down firmly and your hands are away from the cutter.

Swivel buttons hold down the workpiece

Profile

Spindle runs along this edge of the base-board

Recess for workpiece

The jig is firmly screwed to the base-board at regular intervals

solution 5

ROUTER DOVETAIL JIG

This jig is designed for cutting a dovetail on the end of a shelf board so that it will slide into a dovetail channel. The shelf board is positioned between the two underboards so that the end is flush with the top surface of the table. The whole works is clamped, and then the router dovetail bit is put into the guide channel and run past the board end. After doing one side of the dovetail, the bit is run past on the other side. This jig a great idea when you have to cut a pile of shelves.

See also: sliding dovetail / solution 3 / page 52

ABOVE A router alongside a dovetail jig. You can see by the profile of the jig fingers how the dovetail cutter and the straight cutter are used on their respective pieces.

LEFT This simple router jig enables you to cut a dovetail accurately across the end of a board.

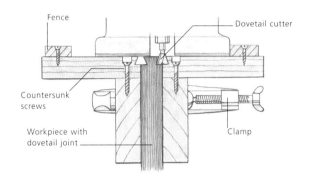

solution 6

ABOVE This jig enables you to drill an identical pattern of holes in a number of parts.

RIGHT This jig enables you to drill a pattern of holes in the face of a board.

DRILLING JIG

This jig is no more than two battens screwed together in an L-shaped section, with a pattern of pre-drilled holes running through one batten. It's an easy-to-make jig, perfect when you need to drill a good many screw holes of the same pattern in a number of parts. In use, you drop the jig onto the edge of the workpiece, check that it's on the right face, clamp it, and then drill the holes. The joy of this jig is that it cuts out a whole lot of measuring and thinking.

See also: dowels / solution 1 / page 60

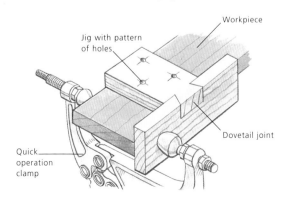

TABLE-SAW PUSH PLANE

Though there is no doubt that the table saw is a useful and efficient power tool, and though it may look harmless enough when the blade is not spinning, it can do truly terrible things to you—you can lose fingers in a twinkling! If you take it for granted and start taking risks, sooner or later you are going to get in trouble. One such risk has to do with trying to cut short lengths of thin stock, with your body leaning over the table, and with your hands near the spinning blade. If you were to lose your balance, or the wood suddenly shoots forward, and you slip … .

The good news is that such risks can be canceled out by using a low-tech item known as a push plane. It is a type of jig, because you can easily make a number of push planes to accommodate and simplify a whole range of tasks. The device has a shaped handle—like that of a hand saw—sandwiched between two or more blocks, with a slot running down their length, wide enough to allow the table saw blade to pass through it, and the end nearest you forming the short leg of a downward L. Described another way, if you were to cut a slot

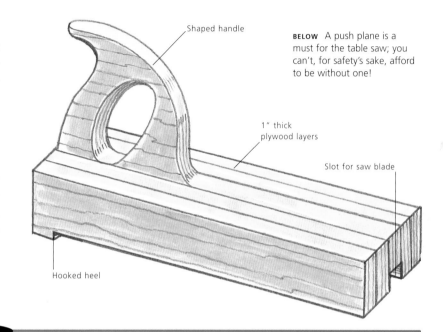

Shaped handle

BELOW A push plane is a must for the table saw; you can't, for safety's sake, afford to be without one!

1" thick plywood layers

Slot for saw blade

Hooked heel

ABOVE A featherboard is one of the easiest jigs to make, and very effective as a safety aid.

FEATHERBOARD

A featherboard is one of those items that looks silly at first sight, designed by who knows who for who knows what. The fact is that it is truly a clever aid that not only guides the wood through the table saw, router or whatever, but also resists kickback. The featherboard shown is a length of ½ in. thick wood about 4 in. wide and 24 in. long, cut off at 45° at one end, and with the angled end sawed at ⅛ in. intervals. In use, the feathers deflect just enough to allow the workpiece through, but then resist kickback.

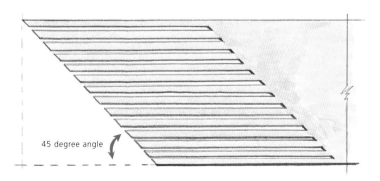

45 degree angle

LEFT The kerfs are at ⅛ in. intervals—so that the resultant feathering is flexible—like the teeth of a comb.